DATE DUE

GAYLORD			PRINTED IN U.S.A.

CHALLENGE
TO
AMERICAN
YOUTH

CHALLENGE
TO
AMERICAN
YOUTH

EDITED BY

Philip Angeles

Macrae Smith Company: Philadelphia

The author wishes to express his thanks to the authors of the essays included in this book for their kind permission to publish their work; and to Robert Taylor, Assistant to the President, University of Wisconsin, for his permission to include the message of the late President Elvehjem.

Preface

A CENTURY that has harnessed the atom and invaded outer space is still groping to find a way for human beings to live together in peace and justice. These are delicate times. The world seems unable to step back from the brink of destruction. Now, more than ever, are we in need of the tempered advice of our wise men. Not only do our young people need to be guided along the steep, tortuous path that lies ahead, but our older citizenry also requires the counsel of enlightened minds.

It is seldom that the thoughts of so many prominent living Americans—prominent in all walks of life—have been combined in one book to light for us a few candles. It has been said that criticism often seeks to find fault with the modern and inspiration only from the ancient. While the writer lives, we rate his ability by his worst performance; when he is dead, we evaluate him by his best. Let us not continue to apply this mistaken criterion. The essential requirement for this book has been that it be itself excellent, and that it give American youth the opportunity to "hear" inspiring ideas, cogently expressed.

In order to form this book, an exhaustive task of communication was established with more than two hundred persons in every field of endeavor. We said, "Public addresses are often pieces of oratory that stir the minds and hearts of men. But notwithstanding eloquence or worth, they are usually filed away in oblivion. Many of these speeches are literary gems that merit a better fate.

PREFACE

They deserve an opportunity to continue to light the paths of men and women of all ages.

"A collection of some of the choicest recent addresses in book form would be a significant contribution toward our national goals."

If this be true; if Americans value the opinions of their own intelligentsia; if Americans desire to learn what their leaders believe regarding vital national and international problems, and want this counsel in print for continued reference, then this book will in some measure satisfy a need.

Cooperation of the distinguished men and women here included is gratefully acknowledged, as is the help of those who, regretfully, could not be so included.

The editor gratefully acknowledges his debt to his wife, Dorene, for her invaluable suggestions and help.

PHILIP ANGELES, PH.D.
Chairman, Department of Modern Languages
Pensacola Junior College
Pensacola, Florida

Contents

CONTENTS

CHALLENGE
TO
AMERICAN
YOUTH

PERSONAL GOALS

Fred L. Whipple

BEFORE the first successful airplane flight had been made, H. G. Wells observed, "All this world is heavy with the promise of greater things, and a day will come, one day in the unending succession of days, when beings, beings who are now latent in our thoughts and hidden in our loins, shall stand upon this earth as one stands upon a footstool, and shall laugh and reach out their hands amidst the stars." That was in 1902.

Now, over sixty artificial satellite objects are being tracked in orbit about the earth, including miscellaneous rocket debris. I say also that some of these objects will remain in orbit for many thousands of years, longer than our historical record.

Seven men have ridden rockets into empty space and have returned to earth successfully; men have circled the entire globe in less than two hours. A man has piloted an aircraft at nearly a mile per second. Satellites have served as communication links between remote points on the earth; they have also repeatedly made pictures of the entire earth's surface and its cloud cover, and then transmitted them back to the ground. Already we have accumulated an enormous body of knowledge about interplanetary space, the high-energy radiations and particles abounding there, and have even "photographed" the sun by means of its X-rays. The moon's majestic serenity has been ruffled by a direct hit and, as John Nemiah puts it, "The moon has at last lost her modesty and shown us her backside."

Soon man will have penetrated some of the major mysteries, not only of the moon, but of Mars, of Venus, and the solar system. He is rapidly accumulating basic knowledge to unravel the ancient strands of time, the evolutionary processes that brought our planet into being. Possibly he will reconstruct or recreate the chemical processes that led to sentient beings and to man himself. No longer will man need to be confined to this cloud-bound planet, or limited in his study of the great universe by this murky and opaque atmosphere that, though essential to his evolution, has nevertheless hampered observation of those vast reaches in time, space and matter of which we and our planet are but a microscopic point. I believe, in short, that man can eventually understand the nature of our universe, its evolution and even its origin, if there be one.

Already our scientific knowledge and our technical skills have left the launching pad in a rocket flight to unpredictable realms of unpredictable power. New energy sources for human use will make fossil fuels, such as oil and coal, seem like matchsticks in a forest. By hydrogen fusion our oceans will eventually become power sources wherein pounds, or even ounces, of water more than equal a ton of coal. Medical progress will conquer essentially all diseases except one that is universally fatal, old age. Science has even penetrated the market place and government. Whereas stockbrokers and politicians may have once consulted astrologers, they now consult astronomers. As Lloyd Berkner has said, "There is hardly anything that man has done that the new science cannot tell us how to do better."

These potentialities in science and technology, if properly used by our world leaders and ourselves, will shrink our globe to at most an hour's travel between the most remote points. Weekend trips from Boston to Tahiti or Australia by rocket aircraft may become commonplace, but probably will still cost a lot. We will be able to control the weather, within limits, and thus outwit Mark Twain, who said that everybody talks about the weather but nobody does anything about it. Certainly we will be able to predict the weather with high accuracy. Food and the comforts of life can be made available to far more people than are now alive. I believe we can, if we choose, make this planet support a hundred to a thousand times as many people as now live on it and this in comfort and security, if not in larger living areas.

We have seen the Industrial Revolution merge into the Scientific Revolution, or is it the Technological Explosion? We are at the beginning of a cultural revolution. Certainly we must learn to live closer and closer together and with greater harmony on this shrinking globe. In his long, long evolutionary travel from amoeba to a thinking being, man has now reached a crossroads that demands a decision. The remarkable new tools and powers resulting from his curiosity and his accumulation and his utilization of knowledge, he can use either destructively or creatively. Because of the powerful weapons that are now available, lack of cooperation on the global scale can result in catastrophe. On the other hand, the potential for secure living and creative expression is truly explosive.

Will man follow his instincts or his reason? Instinct tells him to shrink back within the group whose cultural background matches his own, and within this group to fight aggressively against external groups that seem different or threatening. This instinct has, of course, been a major factor in man's mastery of his environment and, indeed, in his very survival. Now it becomes a veritable hazard. Reason tells him that other men are really like himself—in fact, by fundamental criteria, indistinguishable. If he is to survive and exploit usefully his tremendous powers, he must learn to cooperate on the large-group level as well as he cooperates with his next-door neighbor. This development, along with all the other impacts of the scientific revolution on man's social, religious and political institutions, is what I mean by the cultural revolution, now well under way.

Considering the creative powers man has grasped through modern technology and the scientific method, war, racial discrimination and religious intolerance seem truly absurd— in fact, plain crazy. We already have at hand the means for producing all the food necessary to feed well every human being on the planet. Not only that—we can provide him with good living conditions and the opportunity for self-realization. We could do all this for everyone in a relatively short time if national, political, racial and religious barriers did not stand in the way, and if the population increase could be kept in balance with food production. As we all know, these socio-political problems are extraordinarily complicated and difficult to solve. Instinctive and irrational barriers against theoretical solutions often frustrate all efforts to deal with these human problems.

Yet solutions must be found, and *you* must help to find them. I must tell you with all the earnestness at my command that in the next several decades you—and I mean you, now at a turning point in your lives—will have to exert greater influence on world affairs to determine future events than other generations have wielded before you. We have recently, and I think beneficially, seen our own government turned over to younger hands. The flexibility and imagination of younger minds must be coupled with the experience and wisdom of the race if these remarkable new powers are to be applied for the maximum benefit to man everywhere.

You have seen that there is little place or use for the untrained mind in our kind of world. What lies ahead? How should you proceed, not only for your own personal satisfaction, but as a contributor to the swift developments of today?

I cannot answer these questions for each of you. The questions have different meanings that depend upon your varied abilities and backgrounds. But perhaps I can help a bit. I believe that the most important factor in the future of every man and woman is a clear-cut goal in life. When goals are clearly and courageously enunciated to one's self, the satisfactions—first, in planning, and then in accomplishment—cannot be exaggerated. I use the term "courageously" here with intent, for it is sometimes difficult to discover or to admit to one's self the true nature of one's fundamental desires and aspirations. Now, the basis of motivation is a complicated psychological problem that may be solved practically in the cultural revolution just beginning, but as a layman in this subject I will not venture into such deep waters. Suffice it to say that oftentimes there are enormous barriers to be broken down if a person is to admit to himself the nature of his true goals. Frequently, dominating personalities, whether relatives, friends or associates, lead one to misjudge one's own desires or aspirations. Sometimes it is lack of self-confidence or excessive modesty. On the other hand, of course, the goals should be reasonably realistic. Individuals differ in the degree of their satisfactions with their achievement. Most of us, I believe, should try to remain content not to become President of the United States or head of the new world confederacy. Moreover, we must allow ourselves some flexibility in realizing our aims. Sheer persistence, an admirable trait for a person who has wisely chosen, may become a millstone about the neck of one who has chosen badly. We must temper determination with reason and be brave enough to change our course when experience shows us that we can make no headway in our chosen direction.

Then, too, *success* can become a problem. Herbert Elliott, the greatest mile runner in history, who finally smashed the four-minute mile record, recently said, "Actually, I need a new goal. After you've achieved your goals, you have to sit down and think a while." A sage comment, I believe.

In our culture we should try to enunciate at least two types of goals. One involves career, and the other, the way one wishes to live his life. Some societies, but not ours, clearly delineate the goals of youth in both domains. In India, at least until recently, a young man followed the trade of his father and expected his parents to select a suitable wife who would help him establish a happy home, with relatives and friends forming a compatible, companionable and pleasant social unit. Here, for better or for worse, the problem is more difficult. Our technical progress, by shrinking space and presenting myriad opportunities for work and expression, complicates our choice of aim. If one wishes to give his life value, increased responsibilities for rational action accompany these greater opportunities.

PERSONAL GOALS

The multiplicities of potential for creativity or destruction constitute the strength and, at the same time, the danger in our new world.

In thirty-five years of post-graduate experience as scholar, teacher, citizen and observer, I have learned at least one major thing: the person who knows what he wants clearly and explicitly, and who continuously works towards his objectives, has an amazingly good chance of reaching them satisfactorily, if not always completely. If one has the patience to keep trying, barriers simply melt away under continued, directed pressure. The people who have my greatest sympathy are those who do not know what they want.

Whether your goal be a highly successful career, a creative life, a lazy life, an intellectual life, service to mankind, a happy family, many friends, adventure or whatever, state it to yourself and strive to attain it. You may go further than you dream!

FRED L. WHIPPLE is the Director of the Smithsonian Institution Astrophysical Observatory, Cambridge, Massachusetts. Dr. Whipple is an author as well as an astronomer, having written *Earth, Moon and Planets,* and numerous technical and scientific papers.

TO REACH HIGH PLACES

Crawford H. Greenewalt

FREE expression is one of the characteristics of our society. And the privilege of living in a free society is indeed the greatest privilege that we enjoy as citizens of this country.

Our privileges in this respect did not come easily. To obtain them, our ancestors fought bitter and bloody struggles and, ever since, we have been obliged to exercise eternal vigilance to protect our freedom from encroachment, both from inside and outside our boundaries. And we still serve as missionaries for freedom in other parts of the world. In this spirit, we have engaged in wars to preserve freedom in other countries that wished to retain it for themselves and for their citizens and we extend to other nations, even today, the hopeful hand of a free people.

Freedom is indeed a priceless gift, and I know that there is

nothing in America that is more important or more characteristic of us as a nation. All of the material things we enjoy,
all of our prosperity, all of our spiritual well-being, arise
directly out of the fact that we live in a free society, a society
which meets the tests of spiritual as well as temporal appraisal.

All this came into being many years ago, and yet the great
adventure of entering the free society is in a way experienced
by every one of us as we pass through that vague boundary
that separates childhood and adolescence from maturity. Our
childhood, we might say, is spent in an atmosphere of benign
totalitarianism, with our parents thinking for us, caring for
us and guiding us through the uncertainties of our youth.
And to bring the analogy a bit closer, it can be fairly said
that this period is not without its turbulent side. I suppose
that all of us have felt like starting local revolutions, or at
least our own version of the Boston Tea Party, when parental
pressures seemed a bit too harsh. I can assure you that there
is also the reverse side of the coin, since parents, when their
patience is sorely tried, frequently suspect that what we
might call retaliation in force would lead to greater harmony
and understanding between parent and offspring.

In college, we experience some lightening of authoritarian
repressions, or at least a change in their form, with the
faculty sharing the role of the benevolent despot and sharing
also, I would guess, both the exasperations and the rewards
of temporary dictatorship.

Eventually, however, the period of kindly control comes
to an end. You have before you the exciting experience of
becoming full-fledged citizens in a free society.

You will find that the privileges of such a role cannot be
assumed lightly. Privileges carry with them both responsibilities and restraints—qualities all the more vital in that

they must be shouldered voluntarily and defined in accordance with our own conscience. There are few rules that will offer clear guidance, few laws that will suggest more than minimal standards.

When we speak of freedom, for example, we must realize that it is never absolute, that the art of living harmoniously within even the smallest segment of society requires us to moderate to some degree our desires to do precisely as we please. We must learn to balance the maximum of personal option for ourselves with the corresponding rights of our neighbors.

We see this close at hand in the benevolent institution of matrimony, for it is in marriage that we make our first voluntary renunciation of rights and privileges which until then had been purely within our own whim. The test of a successful marriage, it seems to me, lies in finding a reasonable *modus vivendi* in which each party gives up some, but not too much, of personal idiosyncrasy. When one partner overwhelms the other, or when the struggle for domination creates continual tension, the marriage fails, just as any other human association, faced with similar difficulties, would be counted a failure.

Harmonious relationships, then, require of us an inevitable surrender of personal privilege. Yet individual expression, individual initiative, require just as clearly independent judgment and original conclusions. A satisfactory adjustment to life depends upon a just and artful suiting of one to the other.

Unless you have reconciled yourselves to a hermit's cave or a desert island, your careers and your opportunities will be within the context of human associations, social and professional. Most of you in one way or another will become members of organizations. Your effectiveness will be conditioned largely by how well you learn to live within the organizational environment.

Life within an organization is necessarily a series of compromises in which self-interest is tempered by consideration for others and in which group effort must be enlivened and invigorated by individual performance.

All too often, I am afraid, the requirements of good manners and felicitous associations are interpreted as a brake upon individual expression. Some will respond in angry protest and in outraged dignity, managing meanwhile to alienate the cooperative support essential to any personal achievement. Some will respond by assuming that individual initiative has gone the way of the dinosaur and that refuge lies only in the sanctuary of what is now called "conformity."

Adjustment requires neither brash self-assertion nor unquestioning compliance. It calls rather for a choice of values which recognize that individual aims and organizational goals are thoroughly compatible, and may be achieved with honor both for the individual and the organization with which he is associated.

The organization which disregards individual development does so at its peril. And in this day and age it is equally dangerous for an organization to become the victim of a "conformity" complex among its people. No organization can be anything more than a cross section of the individuals it comprises. For its aspirations will be their aspirations, its accomplishments will be no more than a synthesis of their contributions, whether their position be high or low.

Institutions are less the lengthened shadow of one man, as Emerson saw them, than the conglomerate shadow of many men; as the constellation is the ensemble of its stars, a church is the composite of its congregation, an army the total of its ranks and files, and a corporation the sum of the many talents, skills and efforts embodied in its people.

The important thing is that each of us do his part and do it as well as he can—doing, as Carlyle says, not what lies dimly at a distance, but what sits clearly at hand. In doing so you will find, I think, that there is ample room within our society for individualism, just as there is ample necessity for cooperation. And it is as we learn to distinguish the conformity of behavior with the conformity of thought that we approach the real significance of the term "success."

Success is not a measure of what we are given at birth: it is what we ourselves do with whatever characteristics, either mental or physical, either good or indifferent, with which we are endowed.

We are not all born to reach high places. In physique, intelligence and good looks we have certainly not been created equal. Each of us has certain talents and abilities—some of a very high order, some a good average, some perhaps on the poor side. These natural endowments are the tools with which we must live our lives and with which we must build as sound an edifice as we can. If in the years to come you can look yourselves in the eye and say with complete honesty that you have used your talents to the utmost, you will be successful men and women, quite regardless of the stature you assume in the eyes of the world. Conversely, if you fail that examination, you will fail of real success, no matter how high that stature.

Unfortunately, we have fallen victim in recent years to judgments which employ only the universally obvious criteria, often to the neglect of standards much closer to reality. Shakespeare said four hundred years ago that "the world is still deceived with ornament"; today, I sometimes think, it is even less attentive to the basic truths. For we take life often at its most superficial and conclude that achievement can be measured only in terms of applause or wolf whistles or financial compensation. In so doing, we penalize not only those whose accomplishments are beyond the average, but those of lesser qualifications who may well find in their lives only the sober gratification of reaching their full potential.

To the extent that we apply spurious standards to achievement we weaken ourselves as a nation. The extraordinarily gifted individual may indeed make contributions of singular importance. We in America owe a great debt to many such individuals—to Franklin, to Washington, to Lincoln, to Eli Whitney. But the gifted few do not make a nation any more than a few beautiful blooms make a garden. The proportion of outstanding individuals in any nation at any time would probably be fairly constant; the strength of a particular nation must be determined by the accomplishment of its entire citizenry, at all levels.

The poets and philosophers have admonished us for centuries to set our sights high, to hitch our wagons to a star, to let the reach exceed the grasp. That is all well and good, but too much emphasis on "stars" gives us all too often the feeling that to miss is to fail, when the fact is that failure lies only in complacent contentment. For it is not the reward that supplies the satisfaction; it is the good hard try, win, lose or draw.

Not long ago someone asked me if our organization would not benefit hugely by the addition of a dozen or so men of genius. Well, of course, no one can overestimate the possibilities inherent in human achievement at the genius level. But in the light of reality I was moved to reply that our organization would benefit more decisively not by a dozen extraordinary contributions, but by a ten per cent increase in efficiency and application diffused through all levels and all ranks of our present personnel. For the difference between an organization of the first rank and one of lesser stamp is seldom great. It was Darwin, I think, who noted that men differ less in the total of their capacities than in the degree to which they use them.

If our company is to be more successful than the enterprises with which we compete, it will not be because we have more men of top-flight ability, but rather because *all* of our people are distinguished by a small, positive increment of devotion, dedication or determination. It is such modest differences in individual achievement multiplied by many thousands or millions that distinguish a great company from one that is indifferent and, with equal truth, a great nation from its weaker neighbor.

The important thing is that we bring into play the full potential of each of us, whatever our capacity. If we count ourselves a failure because we do not reach the pinnacle, or because we are engaged in an effort which, for some reason, we do not regard as worth while, then our capacities decline and with them the strength of our total commitment as a people.

What we feel about others reflects most accurately what we feel about ourselves, and self-diagnosed failure, prompted by acceptance of the foot-race concept of life, often breeds envy and bitterness toward those who pass us in the stretch.

Rational thought and a true sense of appropriateness will demonstrate, I think, that what we call success is relative, that there are compensations and satisfactions to be found at all stages, and that the truly successful person is the one who leaves no plain of his talent unfurrowed, no portion of his potential unfulfilled.

In no area is our need for sensitive perception so acute

as in the balance upon which we weigh ourselves and our performance. Alfred North Whitehead, the British philosopher who lectured at Harvard, saw in his long study of historical perspective the applicability of this principle.

"That society flourishes most," he said, "in which men think grandly of their function."

To be a success, think grandly of your function and you will think grandly of yourselves and, in so doing, find rewards for yourselves and progress and greatness for your country.

CRAWFORD H. GREENEWALT is Chairman of the Board of E. I. du Pont de Nemours & Co., and formerly its President. A many-sided man, he recently authored a best-selling book on hummingbirds, for which he also did most of the research and photography.

THE VALUE OF READING

Lawrence C. Powell

It is your *years,* rather than your ears that I seek. I am prepared to be short, to make sense if I can, and, above all, to hold your interest, for I have something to say to you. About a particular Little Package. What's in it? Dynamite to blow you up. Honey to heal you. A fire opal for beauty. A scarf of colored silk. Sea shells for music. River sand to filter impurities. Rose petals. Leaves of grass.

I am not being obscure. You know what I mean by "Little Package." Books, of course. I would be a poor librarian if I did not talk about my stock in trade. I know about books. I have lived with them all my life; have collected a million and a half for my university, and a few for myself; have written some; read many; and, best of all, led other people to read.

You can lead a student to the library—for it has uses not

involving books—but you cannot make him read. However, I shall try, by throwing the book at you. What an explosive stockpile a library is—all those little packages stacked up and awaiting the detonation that occurs when they are touched by hand and eye and mind! And when one of them is unwrapped by the act of reading—for example, Milton's pamphlet on the freedom of the press, the *Areopagitica,* first published in 1644—then the fission and the fallout are more far-reaching than from any atomic split.

Society tells you that sheepskin is synonymous with success. As you gradually level out on the plateau of middle age, most of you will never read anything more difficult than newspapers and magazines.

Now listen, here's my warning to you. If you want to maintain your security and self assurance, stay away from certain books. Don't open that little package if you are afraid of being blown sky-high, or lulled to dreams, or dazzled by beauty. Pandora's Box had nothing on a book.

What book? I'll name a few. Some I've lived with, read, and reread, through youth and middle age. The dangerous books are not the ones the censors try to suppress. An honest book about sex—*Lady Chatterley's Lover,* for example—is not dangerous, either to the individual or to society. I like that story about the Italian printer in Florence who first set *Lady Chatterley* in type, back in 1928. Not a word of English did he know, and when a prudish friend of his, who did know English, warned him that the book was dangerous to morals because of what was done and the words used to tell it, the printer asked for an explanation in Italian. "My faith!" he replied. "We do that every day!"

The dangerous books of American literature are about such things as whales, grass, a pond in the woods, a raft on the river. Poems, essays, novels. Beware of these little packages, these bombs in sheep's binding. They slide down the throat, then explode in the stomach, whereas such obviously revolutionary books as *Das Kapital* and *Mein Kampf* stick in the throat, and if they are swallowed, produce indigestion from their lumpiness. Their time has passed. They are dead.

A book of poems, I said. Walt Whitman's, of course. First published in 1855, in a small edition at the author's expense, with his own portrait as frontispiece, instead of his name on the title page, *Leaves of Grass* has been continuously in print for one hundred and six years. Let me prove for you how alive it is.

Recently we were visited by twenty of the leading educators of Latin America. They saw everything there was to see, and as a final sight our shrine of shrines, the William Andrews Clark Memorial Library, built of marble, travertine, bronze and oak, paid for with copper money from Montana and Arizona. The Clark Library houses the world's greatest collections of John Dryden and Oscar Wilde. Exhibits were arranged of these foreign jewels; but then, just before the guests arrived, I was seized by literary patriotism. Something American was needed. I rushed to the shelf and put out on an open table the first edition of *Leaves of Grass*, and the most beautiful modern edition of the book, the folio printed thirty years ago in San Francisco at the Grabhorn Press.

Then the guests and their wives arrived—university rectors and educators from Argentina, Chile, Uruguay and Brazil. They strolled through the building, exclaiming at the bibliographical wonders on view—John Dryden's autographed letter to his cousin, Oscar Wilde's sad letters from prison, the first editions of *Paradise Lost* and Newton's *Principia Mathematica*. And then the Brazilian Minister of Education, an intense and restless man who had wandered after the group, with eyes glazed from too much sight-seeing—Disneyland, Marineland, Forest Lawn—saw *Leaves of Grass* where I had not so innocently placed it—the little package of the first edition, the big package of the Grabhorn reprint—and, like a hawk dropping on a mouse, he fell on that book; and he came to life as though an electric current had been turned on in an idle motor. He seized the book, riffled the pages, and finding what he was looking for, called everyone around him, and began to read aloud, with a delightful accent:

"Shut not your doors to me, proud libraries,
  For that which was lacking on all your well-filled shelves, yet
     needed most, I bring;
  Forth from the war emerging, a book I have made,
  The words of my book nothing—the drift of it everything. . . ."

"He is our great poet," I said, when the Brazilian had finished.

"Ours too," he insisted. "He belongs to all the Americas. Walt Whitman should be required reading in all the schools, from the primary grades on up. What better textbook for creative living?"

He put the book down. The current went out of him, and he merged with the group.

Open the little package of a paperback Whitman, and read for yourself. If there is any life in you, the current from this book will make you spin and hum like a dynamo. If you don't react to it, you are dead and don't know it, and you will live out your deadly life exactly as surveys show most college graduates to be living, subscribing to the correct magazines, belonging to a book club, absorbing cultural rations along with vitamin pills, and with predigested reading matter in every bathroom.

This, alas, is exactly the way most of you will live, and nothing I say will affect you, today or tomorrow or ever. My hope is that for a few of you my words will be a time-bomb, set to go off one year, five years, ten years hence; and that one summer evening you will be in a drugstore or a supermarket—very successful, with wife and/or husband at home; children; cars; T.V.; hi-fi; magazines—when, loaded with medicament or groceries, you will stop by the rack of paperbacks, and something will happen to you. At long last, this talk will explode, down by your solar plexus, and in desperation, you will spin the rack, seeking those books about grass and whales, about a pond in the woods, a raft on the river.

You will look around, to make sure no one sees you being different, and then you will buy *Leaves of Grass, Moby Dick, Walden* and *Huckleberry Finn,* all for less than a fifth of Scotch. You will put them in your cart with vitamins, cold cream and Kleenex, with the Nescafé, the Purex, the Rykrisp and the soap that floats.

You will go home with your packages of tin and paper, and their contents will be consumed—vitamins, coffee, bleach, fruit, crackers, soap—and only those littlest packages will remain. Those paperbacks. You will reread these works of American literature, finding them as different as you have become different from the student who had to read them for credit; and I hope you will read them with pencil in hand, underlining passages that move you to yes or no. You can do things to your own replaceable paperbacks that you can't —or shouldn't—do to library books.

In this depleting world of ours, characterized by the conventional and the orthodox, by the quickie, the cheapie and the noisy, you will need, and will receive, the life and the light that are in these books. Don't ask me how. This is a miracle of chemistry, whereby the life of a creative writer is not lost when he dies, but is transfused into his book, and gives immortal vitality to *Leaves of Grass, Moby Dick, Walden,* Emerson's *Essays* and *Huckleberry Finn.*

And by another miracle, equally staggering, you can tap this life, at once explosive and consoling, can plug into this source of energy and of renewal, can both dynamite and heal yourself, merely by the act of reading.

What we need to shatter is the mold of conformity into which we settle after the fluid state of childhood. A true university values and teaches thoughtful nonconformity. I do not mean mere eccentricity. In this struggle to find and to be yourself, the great books (neither word is capitalized) can be of help to you.

What makes a book great—a so-called classic—is its quality of always being modern, of its author's—though he be long dead—continuing to speak to each new generation.

"I have written a wicked book," Melville exulted in a letter to his neighbor Hawthorne, after completing *Moby Dick,* "and I feel spotless as the lamb."

Listen to what Emerson said about language: "The short Saxon words with which the people help themselves are better than Latin. The language of the street is always strong." In the eighteen fifties, Emerson hailed Whitman's vitality and vulgarity—qualities which often go together—and I have no doubt that if Emerson were alive today he would be reading *Tropic of Cancer* and *The Catcher in the Rye.*

Unlike journalism, literature can never be written to order. There is no way of foretelling the time or place of the appearance of a masterpiece. The power of a work which elevates it from journalism to literature shocks the conventional and scares the timid. Efforts at censorship only serve to advertise a book. In spite of nervous parents and self-appointed censors, *The Catcher in the Rye* has taken its place as a kind of bible for the present generation. I asked a sixteen-year-old boy what he thought of it. "Man," he said, "I'd do all those things Holden Caulfield did, if I only had the money!"

In the years ahead, you graduates will go to the ends of the earth, and beyond, to the realms of space. Take books with you, those little packages of American literature; you will find them good passports, and good rations: Hawthorne and Hemingway, Mark Twain and Carl Sandburg and Robert Frost, Melville and Steinbeck, Emerson and J. Frank Dobie; the genteel and the vulgar, from Henry James to Henry Miller. Foreigners will judge you by the books in your baggage. The timeless values these authors embody are also without national boundaries. In Africa, Asia and India, as well as in Europe, you will go further on paperback than in a Cadillac.

If we are to triumph in the world struggle, it will be because our ideas, not our arms, are the strongest, and books are the best packages man has ever found to hold his ideas. We should be telling the world that the American way, the revolutionary way of individual rights and freedom and responsibility, promises the fullest development for backward peoples; and the best way to tell our story is by the great books of our American heritage. Let them be translated into every tongue of mankind, printed in paperbacks and sent down the rivers of the world. Huck Finn and his black friend, those children of the Mississippi, will go just as surely down the Congo, the Nile, the Ganges and the Yellow River.

You moon-travelers, put *Walden* in your pocket, if the Air Force will let you; it bulks less, yet weighs more, than

THE VALUE OF READING

War and Peace. Hide *Huckleberry Finn* on your person; it will export better than *Crime and Punishment.*

May there ever be books in your life, for there is life for you in books—the essence of all the lives man has ever lived, from Homer to Hemingway, heroic, tragic, loving, wrapped in little packages for your convenience. Turn the leaves of Whitman and you will find the mystical words with which I close:

> I bequeathe myself to the dirt, to grow from the grass I love;
> If you want me again, look for me under your bootsoles.

> You will hardly know who I am, or what I mean;
> But I shall be good health to you nevertheless,
> And filter and fibre your blood.

> Failing to fetch me at first, keep encouraged;
> Missing me one place, search another;
> I stop somewhere, waiting for you.

And so, fare well, go far.

LAWRENCE C. POWELL is Dean of the School of Library Service of the University of California at Los Angeles. He is the author of numerous books and articles, among the former being *Robinson Jeffers: The Man and His Work* and *The Manuscripts of D. H. Lawrence.*

THE MARKS
OF AN EDUCATED MAN

Rabbi Benjamin M. Kahn

IT seems to me that for many generations past the same gloomy note has been sounded, and still the world and men have continued to survive—in many respects quite creatively. "The multitude of our works is emptiness . . . and the days of our life are vanity . . . and the preeminence of man over beast is naught, for all is vanity," wrote the author of *Ecclesiastes* three thousand years ago in a pessimistic, or perhaps dyspeptic, frame of mind. One of the famed Dead Sea Scrolls, entitled, "The War Between the Children of Light and the Children of Darkness," is a quasi-military description of an imminent terminal conflict between the two opposing forces in civilization. "These are the times that try men's souls," are the first words of the sixteen pamphlets on "The American Crisis" which Tom Paine wrote during the seven-year period following the beginning of the Revolutionary War.

History is full of the dates—sometimes even the time of day—when the world was destined to come to an end.

Similarly, the current tendency to despair of the younger generation and to attribute to its failures the chaos of our time ("It is a shame that youth has to be wasted on young people"), has its roots, too, in ancient history. A Sumerian inscription twenty-five hundred years old declares that "The world is coming to an end. Everyone wants to write a book and the young no longer obey their parents. The world is coming to an end."

"In the United States, when everything else fails," writes Harold Taylor, "the custom is to blame education and its product, modern youth. Since the person who blames education can never be proved wrong, and since we can always count on a succession of young men and women, each of them doing something to outrage the moral sense of a preceding generation, this gives us an endless supply of moral indignation to be generated and distributed throughout the social system. 'The denunciation of the young,' says Logan Piersall Smith, 'is a necessary part of the hygiene of older people. It greatly assists in the circulation of the blood.' "

I do not count myself among either the prophets of doom or the denigrators of our young people. When the prophets of the Bible attacked the vested institutions and the injustices of their age, they did so not in hope that the world would be destroyed, but that their challenge, issued in the name of God, would lead to a re-examination of the standards of man and society.

After twenty-one years of professional work with students on college campuses, I am more heartened than ever before by their growing social idealism and ideological commitments. It now appears that they have rejected oversimplified utopianisms of the thirties; nor are they rendered impotent by the apathy which characterized many people in the fifties. Rather do I see in students the type of active realism which is indispensable if we are to meet the challenge of the sixties. It is, for example, the college student on the undergraduate level who has taken the lead toward democratizing the fraternity system in America. It is the college student who is in the forefront of the great struggle for civil rights, which is being conducted with such dignity and restraint. By far the majority of the applicants for service in the Peace Corps comes from our colleges and universities.

The political disinterest of a generation or two ago has given way to an active participation by thousands upon thousands of college students in organizations which support American political parties and ideologies. Throughout the land, students are joining discussion groups and activist clubs for peace; for the sane use of nuclear energy; for the implementation of social service projects in behalf of the greater community. College students are asking fundamental questions in the fields of religion and ethics, questions which by their penetration and perceptiveness challenge the Golden Calves of American civilization. And their horizons have broadened to include the whole world; in their minds' eye they see all nations, all peoples, all mankind as—even if they don't use the phrase—children of one God.

It should come as no surprise that these new, hopeful insights and commitments should stem from, and find their most fertile soil on, the university campus. For this has been the historic role of the educated man. It is inconceivable that Socrates, who challenged the mores of his time, could have been an "average man." It is, after all, a minority of people, the poets, the artists, the intellectuals, the scholars, who set the tone for the age in which they live and who are responsible for its place in history. During the Dark Ages, when illiteracy and ignorance prevailed in most of Europe, the lamp of learning was kept alight in the monasteries of Christian Europe and in the cultural centers and academies of the Jews and Arabs of Moslem Europe. There were few Sunday painters during the period of the Renaissance, far fewer dabblers in art than we have today; and yet, it was the handful of men like Raphael, Da Vinci and Titian whose work made this period one of the most glorious in the history of art and who helped give it its name.

It is, then, the few, the elite—the educated men, if you will—who have spearheaded the raising of the sights and the preservation of the values of our culture and our civilization.

What are the marks of the educated man?

First of all, he is more than well-informed. "A merely well-informed man is the most useless bore on God's earth," wrote Alfred North Whitehead in his superb series of essays on the Aims of Education. I do not accept the validity of the motto on the masthead of a newspaper: "Give the people the facts and they will act intelligently." I would guess that not every alumnus could pass his senior exams a year or two after his graduation! And yet, though he may forget the fact, the date, the formula, the equation, I have no doubt that his whole outlook and orientation, his judgment and his character, have been shaped by what he has learned and by the way he has been taught. He has achieved, it is the university's hope, a sense of perspective, the ability to distinguish between the trivial and the important, the transitory and the eternal. He has been trained to bring to whatever career or profession he follows the greatest possible assets of initiative, insight and integrity. John Stuart Mill put it this way: "Men are men before they are lawyers or physicians or manufacturers; and if you make them capable and sensible men they will make themselves capable and sensible lawyers or physicians or manufacturers."

The educated man is also he who has, by virtue of his learning and the insights engendered thereby, achieved an independent spirit. In a significant, ofttimes courageous, way he stands opposed to the mass culture, the mob rule, the popular cliché. Sometimes he stands in lonely but splendid isolation. He is not a polished, passive scholar and gentleman who accepts without challenge the so-called respectable traditions of his time. And he is definitely not what Dean Alan Simpson of the University of Chicago defined as "the well-rounded man, who has become the organization man, or the man who is so well-rounded that he rolls wherever he is pushed."

"The true measure of education," wrote George Shuster, former President of Hunter College, "was just this—that it could give a human being for all his life, regardless of the circumstances in which he had to live, imperishable love for great art, great truth, and for profound spiritual insight."

These then, are the marks of the educated man. Yet he must live under no illusions that his academic degree and the American system of education provide an easy way to resolve the problems of his age. In his exciting book entitled *The Teacher in America* Jacques Barzun tells us that "Education is the hope of the world, only in the sense that there is something better than bribery, lies and violence for righting the world's wrongs. If this better thing is education, then education is not merely schooling. It is a life-long discipline of the individual by himself, encouraged by a reasonable opportunity to lead a good life. Education here is synonymous with civilization. A civilized community is better than a jungle, but civilization is a long, slow process which cannot be given in a short course. . . . Free, compulsory education

[38]

is a great thing—an indispensable thing—but it will not make the City of God out of Public School No. 26."

What, then, does the educated man, the college graduate, have to contribute to the easing of the crises of our time, to the clarification of our values, to the reorientation of society?

There are many answers to this difficult question. Let me select from them four which seem to me at this moment of special import and relevance.

The first is the responsibility of the educated man to defend the integrity of the individual in the face of conformity-dominated culture.

Modern man is caught in a conflict between self-expression and cultural uniformity. The word "normal" in such a context means "like everybody else." He is, to use David Riesman's analogy, "other-directed, controlled by the standards of his associates rather than by inner conviction." Therefore, it is his special responsibility, as an inheritor of the robes of the educated man, to defend and to promote the right to be different, the legitimacy of expression of the unpopular idea, the refusal of the individualist to be cast into the common mold, the insistence upon man's right above all to be true to himself.

The second responsibility of the educated man in a morally uncertain world is to stand firm on the principle that an ethical orientation and motivation are indispensable foundations for the future. Some of you may recall a television skit which depicted a stenographer and a junior executive discussing the television quiz show scandals. The young man indignantly proclaimed, in the course of a rather discursive and bumbling conversation, "It's a *moral* issue," to which the stenographer replied by saying, "To me that's almost more important than a *real* issue."

The real issue of our day is that politics, government, social

[39]

action, science, and all the other instruments of civilization, cannot function fruitfully, meaningfully and successfully unless they take primarily into regard the welfare of man and his obligation to his neighbor. "It works" is not an ethical criterion. Our foreign policy, the equality of the Negro in the South, social service projects in Africa, space exploration, should be motivated not by a spirit of competition with rival powers, but by the wish to create an environment in which man's humanity and highest welfare may be realized. This is the ultimate responsibility of each one of us as an individual. When the Prophet Micah proclaimed, "It hath been told thee, O man, what is good; and what doth the Lord require of thee but to do justly, to love mercy and to walk humbly with Thy God," he addressed man, everyman, in the singular person and in a singular sense.

Who will inherit the earth? "Thy people, when they shall all be righteous," answered Isaiah.

Thirdly, the educated man must help develop a new concept of freedom for our day. Freedom should mean not just the absence of restraint or the presence of economic opportunity. Freedom means the freedom to be one's self; freedom means the control and mastery of one's self as well as one's environment; freedom means the ability of man to surpass himself—"the power to live spiritually, to rise to a higher level of existence. Who is free? The creative man who is not carried away by the streams of necessity, who is not enchained by processes, who is not enslaved to society itself," says A. J. Heschel in *God in Search of Man.*

Freedom means, above all, the choice which man makes not to yield to the so-called inevitable, not to be resigned to things as they are. The real slavery of the people in Egypt, a Biblical commentator of old explained, was not that the people suffered under tyranny, but that they accepted it without protest. In Eugene O'Neill's very moving play *Long Day's Journey Into Night,* the mother, in a moment of genuine despair and self-abnegation, mournfully declares, "None of us can help the things life has done to us. They are done before you realize it and before you know it, you have lost your real self forever." At that moment she ceased to be free.

Finally, the educated man will bring to the world in which he lives a sense of perspective and a conviction of purpose. His knowledge of history, his understanding of the past, his familiarity with the social forces of society, provide him with the equipment to fit current events into the framework of eternity, to judge the present in the light of the past and in reference to the potentialities of the future. It is this insight which, when communicated to his fellow men, will prevent them from losing sight of their goals in the preoccupations of everyday effort and conflict. Huston Smith, in *The Purpose of Higher Education,* tells the story of an Armenian named Joe, who had a prize lamb which he loved dearly. One day his neighbors decided to take the lamb away from him, at which Joe put the lamb into the center of his one-room house, locked the doors, and proceeded to fire on his neighbors alternately from the east window and the west window. Each time as he moved from the east to the west and back, he tripped over the lamb, until finally in exasperation he thrust the lamb out of the door, closed it and locked it, and continued shooting! . . . When the goals of man's existence are in danger of being lost, then especially must the educated man seek to preserve the sense of perspective and of purpose which alone confer meaning on man's search.

This is, as I see it, your role, your responsibility, your privilege, as you complete the first stage of your education into men and women. I think that all this can be summarized in a word which had its origin in the Bible, the concept of mission. Let me read to you what Professor Clinton Rossiter defined as the mission of America—which is ultimately your mission, too:

> We have been, like the children of Israel, a "peculiar treasure." Upon us destiny has bestowed special favor; of us it has therefore asked special effort. Because men like Washington and Lincoln sensed this grand truth and acted consciously upon it, we have counted more heavily in history than our size and wealth, however majestic, would seem to have warranted.
>
> We have lost the sense of mission of our early years, and yet we need this sense more desperately than ever today.
>
> We need it because we stand at one of those rare points in history when a nation must choose consciously between greatness and mediocrity.

The nation is people—people of all classes, racial strains, national ancestries, economic and geographic stratifications, interests and abilities. The glory of mankind is that each man is unique. And yet, all men possess and are possessed by the same dream—of living together in peace, security and meaningfulness. This dream, I am convinced, is a dream of greatness, not a delusion of grandeur.

To articulate the dream, to define ways of realizing it, and to lead men towards its fulfillment, this is the unique opportunity—the mission, if you will, of the educated man.

I rather think that it was this sense of mission which President Roosevelt had in mind when he read to the United Nations on Flag Day, 1942, a beautiful and eternally relevant prayer by Stephen Vincent Benét:

> God of the free, we pledge our hearts and lives today to the cause of all free mankind.
>
> The spirit of man has awakened and the soul of man has gone

forth. Grant us the wisdom and the vision to comprehend the greatness of man's spirit, that suffers and endures so hugely for a goal beyond his own brief span. Grant us honor for our dead who died in the faith, honor for our living who work and strive for the faith, redemption and security for all captive lands and peoples. Grant us patience with the deluded and pity for the betrayed. And grant us the skill and valor that shall cleanse the world of oppression and the old base doctrine that the strong must eat the weak because they are strong.

Yet most of all grant us brotherhood, not only for this day but for all our years—a brotherhood not of words but of acts and deeds. We are all of us children of earth—grant us that simple knowledge. If our brothers are oppressed, then we are oppressed. If they hunger, we hunger. If their freedom is taken away our freedom is not secure. Grant us a common faith that man shall know bread and peace—that he shall know justice and righteousness, freedom and security and equal opportunity and an equal chance to do his best, not only in our own lands, but throughout the world. And in that faith let us march toward the clean world our hands can make.

Rabbi BENJAMIN M. KAHN is the National Director of the B'nai B'rith Hillel Foundation, and a distinguished educator, scholar and author. He is co-author of the recent *Exploring Religious Ideas: The Great Western Faiths.*

THE PURSUIT OF TRUTH

Henry L. Ashmore

No country in the world has ever placed such great faith in formal education as the United States of America, and no country has ever tied itself so inextricably to its belief as has the nation in which we live. We have decreed that every child shall have access to the public schools; we have devised laws and regulations which literally force a person to attend some type of formal school until he reaches a certain age; we have spent huge sums to insure free education; and we have placed a monetary premium upon the possession of a high degree of learning. Yet there are those today who, recognizing our devotion to the cult of education, steadfastly maintain that our system is a failure, our end results are perverted, and our money is being wasted.

People have been criticizing the education endeavors of men for centuries, and will be for centuries to come. This is particularly true in a democracy.

However, I have no intention of trying to measure the success of our system now; rather, I would like us to seek, instead, the measure of education for the individual. You find yourselves in the enviable position of having finished a course of what is formally called "higher education." Whatever your plans for the future might be, one thing is certain: Individually, and as a group, you are literally stepping into tomorrow. And as you make this inevitable step, how much better equipped are you as a result of your experiences? What is the measure of your education?

As we seek to determine the measure of an education, I would ask you to make this evaluation an intense, personal thing. Apply these ideas to yourself as our minds meet in common cause:

1. The first real measure of an education is whether there is real and creative use of the knowledge you possess, and not just merely an accumulation of assorted, or even unassorted, facts. True wisdom is not the accumulation of data, but the ability to make intelligent use of such data. Because of the rapid technological changes now taking place in our culture, knowledge quickly becomes obsolete; therefore, a person depending upon knowledge alone cannot long function successfully in our society. The individual, however, who can forcefully and competently make creative use of his knowledge is the individual who can claim with incontrovertible logic that he is truly educated. I believe it was Kenneth Winebrenner who stated that the slow thinker who can finally come up with an idea of his own is more important to the world than a walking encyclopedia who hasn't learned how to use the information productively.

2. The second real measure of education is what a person

possessing it has—because of his education—done for others. Contrary to our materialistic philosophy so evident today, education should not be evaluated in terms of what it does for the individual possessing it. Such a fortunate person should be inspired to show his reverence for life by substantially and materially contributing to it. In essence, every educated person should be willing to sacrifice at least a portion of his life in order that other lives might be benefited. If the end result of a formal education must be reduced to the baseness of what it does selfishly to enhance the life only of the one possessing it, then I believe the original will of God has been frustrated, and that a synthetic education has perforce superseded a real education.

Horace Mann, that eminent educator of an early day in American history, summed it up when he said, "Young man, be ashamed to die until you have done something for the benefit of your fellow man."

Dr. Albert Schweitzer, in speaking of his long and wonderfully useful life, had this to say: "One thing I know: The only ones among you who will be really happy are those who will have sought and found how to serve."

3. The third real measure of an education is whether it has created within the individual possessing it a steady and equitable set of values upon which he can predicate his thoughts, his desires, and his actions. We are apparently living in a world sick with the cancer of immorality, drugged with the hedonistic philosophy that we must, at all costs to our basic and fundamental natural desire to respond to original goodness, satiate our own sensual feelings. We have more mental patients

today than ever before, and yet our educational level is the highest it has ever been. Youths coming into my office seemingly possess no fixed, nor even fairly rigid, set of standards or values; or at best, the principles upon which they act are hazy and vacillating. Plato held to the premise that to know is to believe, and to believe is to act. Yet many today do not seem to know, to believe, to act.

It is a tragic and disconcerting thing to see a person without the stabilizing force of a clearly defined set of values. I would state unequivocally that a person who has a formal massing of facts, but has not the wisdom to ferret out his own code of behavior clearly and concisely, based upon a deliberate examination of real values, is not an educated man.

True education would bring peace to the tormented mind and personality through the development of a distinguishing set of values, which would permeate the entire personality of an individual and would dictate the thought process of every compartment of his mind.

4. The fourth real measure of education is the obvious presence of a consuming desire to seek for truth, and having found truth, to accept it and act upon it. Unfortunately, it is much easier to search for truth than it is to accept it and act upon it. However, the truly educated mind would forever be disquieted, restless and hungered if it were not constantly engaged in the never-ending search for truth. But having found some bit of truth, the educated mind must necessarily examine it, embrace it, and eventually weld itself inextricably to it.

Gotthold Lessing, the noted German philosopher, once wrote, "If God were to hold before me in His left hand eternal truth, and in His right the ever present impulse to seek for truth, and say, 'Choose,' I would fall before His right hand and say, 'Father, give, for pure truth, after all, is for Thee alone.' "

There is an ancient legend concerning a philosopher who spent his life in pursuit of truth. After years of searching he heard that truth had been discovered in the bottom of a certain well. Rushing to the well, he looked down into it. Seeing his own reflection mirrored in the still waters, he shouted, "Truth! At last I have found you!"

Unfortunately, this is the conception most of us have of truth—simply a reflection of what we are or what we already believe. This is not what I am emphasizing tonight; rather, it is the opposite. Being truly educated, we must be willing to accept, and incorporate as part of our very being, truth as we find it.

Jesus said, "God is a spirit, and we must worship Him in truth and in spirit."

5. The fifth real measure of an education is whether it enables a person to contact, communicate with, and come to accept completely his divine creator. There would be those who would disagree violently with me on this criterion. That is as it may be, for I would not engage in endless generalities and pointless contentions. Suffice it to say that to me it is as Wordsworth said: "We did come trailing clouds of glory from heaven, our home, and our souls will wander with increasing loneliness until we come to some satisfactory form of understanding with our God." If education does not act as a catalyst in this search, it has failed us.

I hope education will be a compelling force in your life until you, like Francis Thompson in his poem, "The Hound of Heaven," can say, in speaking of God:

THE PURSUIT OF TRUTH

I fled Him, down the nights and down the days;
I fled Him, down the arches of the years;
I fled Him, down the labyrinthine ways
Of my own mind; and in the mist of tears
I hid from Him, and under running laughter.

Until you, like Thompson, give in to the force of God and hear Him say:

I am he whom thou seekest;
Thou dravest love from thee, who dravest me.

To sum up the true measure of education, I should like to paraphrase, with proper apologies, Kipling's "If."

If you can make creative use of your knowledge, while others around you are simply storehouses of facts;

If you can devote some portion of your life to serving others, while most serve only themselves;

If you can develop a set of moral values based upon truth, while others around you are lacking in such values;

If you can spend your life searching for truth, and finding truth, embrace it;

If you can come face to face with your God, and surrender your will to His perfect will;

Then you will be a man, my son, and what is more, you will be an educated man.

DR. HENRY L. ASHMORE is President of the Pensacola Junior College, Pensacola, Florida. A leading Southern educator, he has written many articles and is a recognized authority in his field.

TEST OF AN EDUCATION

Margaret Culkin Banning

THERE is a statement in this country which is becoming a
cliché. It says, "You can't get anywhere today without a
college degree." This is an arrogant statement—untrue of
course (only one half of high school students go to college)—
but there is no doubt, as many recent surveys have shown,
that the drive toward more education has strong occupational
and utilitarian motives. Going to college as a means to improve socioeconomic status presently dominates the purpose
of great numbers of college-going young people and the parents who send them to college. This trend is fed by the increasingly technical demands of the work-world, the specialized training programs of the armed services, and the rising
level of general education of American parents.

A college degree carries with it great advantages and
usually preferment, and these can be calculated. But a col-

lege degree does not carry a price tag because in the mixture of elements which result in a degree there are some beyond price. Some are not for sale. Some never will be used in earning a living but will be invaluable to a good life. They are not present in each individual in the same strength.

I have wanted for some time to protest the cliché that I have mentioned and the tendency to put a market price on a degree. I am aware that a person with a Master of Arts degree usually commands a higher salary than one with a Bachelor of Science degree, because he has more to communicate, more information or skill to use as tools. But salaries, whatever they may be, are not the tests of education. They are its proper earnings.

The tests of an education which I should like to put before you for consideration are more intangible. The first one is the ability to recognize and to use source material. The second is a proper balance between ideas and possessions. The third I would call reasoning power. There are some "naturals," some wise people who, without formal education, meet these tests most adequately. But there are not many, and surely not enough.

Concerning the first test, of sources, the very spirit of knowledge is that you must base your conclusions on adequate grounds. You must make sure that you are going to the real sources of knowledge, discovering what the real facts are and how trustworthy the authority which states them, before you move on to the next process, which is the process of clear thinking. An educated person does not make a judgment on a situation or a person because he has "heard" somewhere but doesn't "remember who said it." What he has heard is measured by the validity of the source, or he does not use the material in work or life.

The second test of an educated person is that he or she

values ideas, which often he can not sell, as well as personal accumulations of possessions. He never thinks of the world as his oyster. He knows—he has learned and seen during his years of study—that there are areas, scattered all over the world today, where people care more for thought than they do for new cars. Colleges, universities, libraries, laboratories, proving grounds, some homes, many student dormitories, have values which are not those of the market place. This is the mark a degree puts or should put on the individual. You are not—should not be—commercial.

Thirdly, the educated person has learned to reason, that subtle process which is the characteristic of the leader, the cultivated man or woman. Amid all our demand for a general, man-made and mass-distributed freedom, the educated person already has set himself free because he can reason and no one can prevent him from doing so. He is not helplessly prisoned, like the victim of prejudice or the victim of ignorance.

They are simple attributes, these tests of an education. We apply them not once, on graduation day, but continually, unless educations fall into disuse or are corrupted. The constant application of the tests is a very healthy practice. An educated person should not make a snap judgment, unless by chance or long effort he is so well-informed and so familiar with the best source material on a particular subject that he needs only an instant for clear, unbiased decision. He can not yield to rumor nor to mob psychology if he lives up to his education.

And how to live up to it? Long ago William James said, "The best claim that a college education can possibly make on your respect, the best thing it can aspire to accomplish for you, is this—*that it should help you to know a good man when you see him*. In this very simple way does the value of our class define itself: *we, more than others, should be able to choose the worthier and better leaders."*

That was over fifty years ago, before either great world war, and what some of us have seen during that half century proves that James was very wise in what he said. Most of the terrible tragedies during these years have been simply because people did not choose the worthier and better leaders, because bad leaders corrupted and misled the uneducated and disadvantaged. Hitler, Mussolini, Stalin—add them up. There are plenty in Europe and Asia, and we have them also in the United States.

For, lest we don't see the mote in our own eye, how about that darkening period in our own national life only a few years ago when suspicion and calumny were so prevalent that students in universities became afraid to join organizations that were perfectly harmless? Senator McCarthy was no genius, clever and unscrupulous though he was. The fault was that educated people, like ourselves, did not demand worthier and better leaders, and let a man like that attain temporary power. McCarthy did not meet the educational tests of sources, of reasoning, of belief in ideas.

Since my own college days, I have always lived in a world whose economy, thought and action were conditioned by two things—war (in fact or threat) and the study of peace. The study of peace has become steadily more important, more reasonable, more engaged in by great and honorable people —and this even in times when war was going on. And the unanimity with which people in all nations have turned to education as their best hope is encouraging and uplifting.

This clinging to education in times of national danger and tragedy has been significant in the last years. Once in England, in 1942, when the bombs were falling and nothing had been restored or repaired, I happened to attend a session

[53]

of Parliament. I had a little free time between a couple of factory inspections and wanted to see how the heads of government looked and acted. It was a time when the war outcome was uncertain. But the discussion in Parliament that day was not about battles but about education. One member rose to say that the interest in education just then was stronger in Great Britain than it had been at any other time in the nation's history. They knew of course that thousands of their finest men and women were being killed and in their grief they were thinking of replacing them by emphasizing education in groups who had never had too much of it. One member suggested converting aerodromes into good schools and vocational centers after the war was over, which would give a great number of young people the privileges that wealthy families had previously enjoyed. To my thinking, it was that sort of attitude of mind which saved Great Britain. It was the instinctive sense that it must preserve the most important things, such as education, though buildings and people were being crushed every day.

In Austria four years later, things were hanging in ruins. I was on a job for UNRRA. In the parks there were people who looked insane from shock. Food was so scarce that horsemeat was a treat. Everything was rationed. The university none the less was in session. The students had a meal of soup and bread in the morning and studied until their strength was exhausted, then fell asleep until the next day.

When I was in Moscow not long ago, my greatest encouragement for the future of the Soviet Union and so, to some extent, our future too, came from visits to the universities. True, they are under government control and the government dictates the jobs that its subsidized students may take. But as the university students flocked around—as they flock around all Americans—it was not just because of curiosity about my shoes and clothes. They were looking, as students always do, for source material. I was a primary source. In Russia they are fairly far advanced in the second test of educated people, for most of them do not value material things as much as ideas. But the third test shows them badly lacking. Their minds are closed in many respects. They are not flexible. Their reasoning power is inhibited by prejudice. Yet there must be thousands of cracks in those closed minds through which true education can enter.

The wars have done great harm but they have changed the hopes and ideals of the whole world in some ways for the better. There is more rethinking about political and economic life now than there was in the previous hundred years. During the nineteenth century and on until the eve of the First World War a set of historical conditions created a pattern of world society which was highly favorable to the Western nations. For nearly a century the peace of the world was maintained by a rough balance of power in Europe and by the supremacy of the European empires in the rest of the world. As the industrial revolution transformed first Great Britain, then Western Europe and then the United States, there were few political obstacles to an immensely rapid extension of their economic interests, their investments and their trade all around the world.

"The truth is," says Barbara Ward, "that, after two World Wars, the whole framework of the older order has been destroyed. No balance of power is conceivable in Europe without an American influence (presence) simply because Russia has outgrown everyone else. The entire colonial system has vanished in fifteen short years. All Asia and most of Africa are virtually independent. China is mobilizing into what may be the greatest single organized system of national power the world has ever seen."

[55]

Why fling such facts into a message to young people? Because no one believes that a balance of power is conceivable without America in it. Because in America the educated people should choose "worthy leaders." Because there is a definite attempt to *think out, reason out,* new balances, new plans; and the Americans most capable of thinking must sit in on these.

Europe is full of meetings. Recently when I was a delegate to the Atlantic Congress in London, which was a very serious and sobering affair, we became conscious of other groups meeting in Sweden, in Holland, in Luxembourg, trying to think out special problems. Too many meetings, some people said in confusion. But meetings are better than battles. In this one I listened to a great number of eminent people— prime ministers, princes, the heads of mass communication in the United States and Great Britain (David Sarnoff and the Earl of Bessborough), professors from Oxford, lawyers from Washington and New York—courteously and to the point of fatigue trying to adjust points of view. It was tremendously encouraging, because it was obvious that the best minds were at work on these problems. These were educated volunteers.

But what did they accomplish? They are laying the foundations of thought, sifting true sources of information from prejudiced ones, as educated people must. They are trying to, in some way, balance ideas and possessions. They are trying to reason out not one but hundreds of answers to current problems.

It is in such good soil *your* education has a chance to flourish. One of the dramatic moments of Congress in recent times came when, because Adlai Stevenson could not be present, his place was filled by Dr. Mordecai Johnson, the president of Howard University in Washington. He is colored, of course, a large, beneficent man, and he began his talk by saying, "We have been hearing much talk about the under-developed people of the world. I am one of those, an American Negro. My father and mother were slaves. My father, when he was freed, became a minister. He used to say to us, 'You must stir up your minds'—and when he became very ardent about something, he would say, 'You must stir up your pure minds' "—which is one of the quotations I brought home to keep.

There is much work that needs doing. The world is confused and will continue to be confused because events are moving so fast. Education is going to be prevalent all over the world and I am not speaking merely of literacy.

This does not mean that education will follow a common pattern throughout the world. We wouldn't want that, nor work for it. The intellectual independence of the colleges and universities and the specialization within them combine to exclude the formulation by the university authorities of even the free countries of anything approaching a common doctrine.

But it is at the college level that, in a free society, an elite is formed, capable of assimilating the essential values of civilization, and of acquiring expert knowledge of political and economic systems and contemporary problems of international relations. The majority of those who are to govern, lead and teach within their national communities in the future pass through the universities. It is also to the universities and the institutes of technology that governments look for scientific research in all fields and for the qualified technicians needed for defense, industry and medical science in the nuclear age.

This is where decent rapport and a link with Russia which we can trust could develop. In the progress of the last forty years Russia has given education first place in its social order. It is still not released from political control but many, many people feel that it will break free one of these days. In another fifty years educated people will be honored not only in Western Europe and a few centers of cultures in the other continents but in every country of the world.

This will change your lives, give you great opportunities and demand—pretty stiffly—that you measure up to them. Not just because of the money you can earn after you get a college degree, but by your ability to choose those worthy leaders—or, better yet, your ability to become one of them.

It hardly matters what your field is—business and economics, social science, French, psychology, sociology, elementary education, geology—each has a growing usefulness in a developing world, each a duty in addition to the personal gain of income. No one disregards that. We are constantly trying to put new securities around the American family. But the additional usefulness, the dignity, the honor, the *pride*, of being an educated person is what I have tried, in this brief message, to urge on you, because you are greatly needed.

MARGARET CULKIN BANNING is one of America's best-loved authors, and a poet as well. Her novels, serials and stories have appeared in almost every major magazine in the United States, as well as in book form.

CONSERVATION:
PHYSICAL AND SPIRITUAL

Stewart L. Udall

On one of his annual visits to Washington, the late Robert
Frost voiced a poet's complaint that there was too much haste,
and too little time to think, in our Nation's capitol. Sometimes it is wise to realize, he told some of us, "that time is
not of the essence."

I could today, as would befit a Cabinet Officer, paint current events on a broad canvas in an attempt to underscore
the nature of the crises we will surely face next year—and
the next. However, in his Inaugural Address, President Kennedy outlined our plight—and our hope—with such concise
eloquence that if I had my wish each of you would carry with
you, and periodically read and reread, this challenging document.

In this speech the President referred to "a new generation

of Americans born in this century" granted "the role of defending freedom in its hour of maximum danger." And it was plainly your generation—more than any other—which the President challenged to "ask not what your country can do for you—ask what you can do for your country."

My department of government is one of the few that is not preoccupied with the task of holding the dark forces in the world at bay. We have the happy function of planning the future of America and working to conserve the natural resources which sustain its life. Consequently, conservation is my theme, and I should like to discuss both the conservation of man, and the conservation of his environment.

Never before has man been so at odds with his environment as we are today in America. In the short span of a hundred years—the century that bridges our great westward expansion and the present day—we have created forces hostile to nature that, given full sway, will in time make us strangers in our own land.

A poet has written of our continent, "The land was ours before we were the land's," and as one surveys the developments of the past two decades, one is driven to the conviction that the land that we and our forebears knew will not be "ours" unless we arrest the forces that would alter and blight it and despoil its fruits.

Because so much of what is happening inside America is drowned out by the clamor of an embattled world, this is a Quiet Crisis—but one which should concern every American nevertheless.

The elements of the Quiet Crisis of conservation are urban sprawl, polluted rivers and lakes, disappearing open space, overcrowded parks, a vanishing shore line, the exploitation of the few remaining portions of this country's wilderness, the threatened extinction of wildlife, and dwindling opportunities for the outdoor experience that has had a profound influence on our national character.

Each element by itself represents, at this stage, no more than a serious inconvenience. But, taken together, they add up to an environment that threatens the wellsprings of our national life.

The history of every civilization, from the Byzantine Empire to the British Empire, is in large part the chronicle of man's emotional and physical relationship to his land and, through the land, to himself and his fellow citizens.

And so it was and is with America.

We found a virgin continent of awesome proportions, with magnificent landscapes and seemingly inexhaustible natural resources. A good many of the qualities which we like to think make up our national character—humility, daring, and inner strength, to name a few—came from testing ourselves against a rugged and demanding natural environment.

Sherwood Anderson had this in mind when many years ago he wrote to Waldo Frank:

Is it not likely that when the country was new and men were often alone in the fields and the forest they got a sense of bigness outside themselves that has now in some way been lost. . . . Mystery whispered in the grass, played in the branches of trees overhead, was caught up and blown across the American line in clouds of dust at evening on the prairies. . . . I am old enough to remember tales that strengthen my belief in a deep semireligious influence that was formerly at work among our people. The flavor of it hangs over the best work of Mark Twain. . . . I can remember old fellows in my home town speaking feelingly of an evening spent on the big empty plains. It had taken the shrillness out of them. They had learned the trick of quiet. . . .

But how do you measure yourself against traffic jams, industrial squalor, smog, and sprawling subdivisions? And if we do try to measure ourselves, what can the verdict be but that we find ourselves wanting?

If man were an economic animal only, we Americans would have to be the happiest of tribes.

We are prosperity's children, in an economy of abundance where few physical needs must go unmet and luxuries abound.

Yet if our contemporary nonfiction is a mirror of ourselves —and I believe that what a society writes about itself is a good indicator of how it feels about itself—then we are a generation of Ugly Americans, Wastemakers, Hucksters, Organization Men, Lonely Crowds and Operators.

At no time has a society achieved as much as we have with as little satisfaction in its achievement and with as much doubt about the future. Clearly in advancing so far so fast we have lost essential values.

It is plain to me that one of the vital things we have lost is our relationship with our land—our feel for and love of the land on which we live.

To achieve the material things of an urbanized and industrialized society we have ignored, denied, exploited and misused our land with such single-minded zeal that to an alarming degree we have succeeded in alienating ourselves not only from the land but from ourselves.

For no matter how urbanized and industrialized we have become, man—the all too recent animal—is biologically and fundamentally rooted in the land.

No one has summarized our loss more eloquently than has Wallace Stegner, the distinguished novelist, who recently wrote in a letter:

CONSERVATION: PHYSICAL AND SPIRITUAL

Something will have gone out of us as a people if we ever let the last remaining wilderness be destroyed, if we permit the last of our forests to be turned into comic books and plastic cigarette cases, if we drive the few remaining members of the wild species into zoos or extinction, if we pollute the last clean air or dirty the last clean streams or push our paved roads through the last of the silence.

Not many people are likely any more to look upon what we call progress as an unmixed blessing. Just as surely as it has brought us increased comfort and more material goods, it has brought us spiritual losses and it threatens to become the Frankenstein that will destroy us.

I hope that you have gathered from my remarks that I attach urgency to need for new thinking on conservation in this country. The chief reason is that whereas in earlier times conservation concerned itself only with wildlife and natural resources, today man himself must become the object of conservation.

We are changing our environment so drastically—so unfavorably—that we must act to preserve the green face of America in order to conserve the resources of the human spirit as well as our natural heritage.

If our growth in the years ahead is wisely planned we will give far more attention than heretofore to the uses to which we put our water and land. In some sections of our country we already face a water crisis of serious proportions. Already the future of some of our river basins hinges on the water conservation practices and programs that are adopted.

What kind of lives we will lead in the future depends to a large degree on what kind of an environment we create for ourselves, on how we treat our land and its resources of water, air, forests and landscapes. If your generation makes the wrong decisions in this area it will surely do so at its peril.

If the times require new conservation ideals and practices, a sense of balance also dictates, and necessity demands, a program of human conservation which will add a new dimension to citizenship and enable each of us to serve ourselves, and the common welfare, by savoring the worth of the individual and making the highest and best use of his innate potential.

However, we can successfully evolve such a program only if we are willing—as the wise conservationist is willing—to live *with* our basic nature, and, as "naturalists" of the science of man, to provide an environment where excellence can flourish and merit have its just reward.

Yet we can accomplish this only if we have a constant infusion of new ideas and new ideals, and we have come to expect our universities to play the largest role in this process of renewal and re-creation.

A democracy by its very nature must lay a heavy wager on the individual—and on the long haul. However, it is part of the geography of our hope that men and women will attempt great things and act in concert for high causes once they are convinced the survival of their civilization is at stake.

The most dangerous illusion we must wrestle with is the myth of automatic progress (and its implicit denial of the individual responsibility) which has fostered among our people a superiority complex that gravely weakens our purpose. The quickest way for us to lose all is to proceed on the easy assumption that we will be "saved" by a new scientific discovery, some feat in outer space, or fortuitous strokes of personal leadership by our public men.

The true political process of our country is a much more subtle mechanism than even the politicians will concede.

Each of you must play a part—some at the center, some at the fringe—in forging the decisions which will decide our future. The individual is the "maximum leader" in our society, and whether this role is a public or private one—and I would hope that yours would encompass both—the stamina and wisdom he summons to the task would decide the course of the race we run.

The quiet men have an equal place in the sun with public men under our system. And those of you who by instinct choose to play this part have your philosopher in William James who wrote long ago:

I am done with great things and big things, great institutions and big successes, and I am for those tiny invisible molecular moral forces that work from individual to individual, creeping through the crannies of the world like so many soft rootlets, or like the capillary oozing of water, yet which, if you give them time, will rend the hardest monuments of men's pride.

This, no less than a national election, is a valid description of the democratic process at work. Therefore, it should be plain that if we want a nation where quality counts, where the national purpose will have support, we must constantly re-examine the relationship between man and society, between our private lives and our public responsibilities.

There are many areas of life where our values might be reoriented.

I would suggest more Americans must make service rather than status their personal goal—and the initial response of our young people to the Peace Corps idea of President Kennedy would indicate there is a much larger reservoir of idealism in our country than many of us have realized, and gives promise that new symbols will replace the old in our scheme of values.

Then again we can change the flavor of our national life if we will belatedly give to the poets and philosophers and scientists and educators and public servants who are the wise men and great teachers of our age the esteem and sway they deserve. Once we fully succeed in enlarging the dialogue between these men and their fellows it will surely release new sources of inspiration among our people.

We must also make a conscious commitment to individual excellence in this country and make it a part of our everyday lives. The quality of American life, and the performance of our country, will in the long run depend on our sense of the excellent, for every time we honor the second-rate, reward the shoddy, or celebrate the foolish we weaken the fiber of our strength. There is in government service today what one of my Cabinet colleagues calls "a crisis of talent," and it inhibits at every turn the achievement of our policies. There simply are not enough able people to go around to enable us to do our best as a country. We have learned that second-rate men should be left at home, and today no one is "doing more for his country" than those men and women of first-rate ability who are serving us well in difficult assignments around the world.

We must take caution that our trades and businesses and professions do not become mere exercises in "getting and spending," but rather offer opportunities to make vital contributions to a complex society, and to help secure a better life for men everywhere. The late Dr. Thomas Dooley must have his emulators in all walks of life if we are to keep alive our finest traditions.

Finally, we must develop a deeper concept of grace—and with it a new respect for our fellow men that admits no invidious attitudes and makes us instinctively weigh the rights of others in the scales alongside our own.

CONSERVATION: PHYSICAL AND SPIRITUAL

Go forth, then, and take your place in the ranks and let your self-fulfillment be, in part, the fulfillment of the high and vital purposes of your nation.

STEWART L. UDALL, United States Secretary of the Interior, is a veteran of World War II (Air Force), an ex-Congressman (Arizona) and a member of a distinguished Mormon pioneer family. He is a living testimonial to the "strenuous life."

A NEED
FOR BALANCED THINKING

Clark R. Mollenhoff

WITHIN a period of the last few years, there has been what
seems an unprecedented pattern of exposure of corruption in
our society. It has been accompanied by considerable dis-
illusionment on the part of young people, as well as many
older people. There are times when it has seemed that every
segment of society was filled with corruption, and in some
cases dominated by it.

There were the major labor scandals centering on some
of the largest and most powerful trade unions. There were
the incidents where officials of some of our largest businesses
were involved in criminal price fixing. There were countless
incidents of police in league with burglars, and there was
a large number of college basketball players caught taking
bribes to shave points. There has been a steady pattern of

investigations revealing high government officials in improper activity or "conflicts of interests."

In the face of problems that have seemed to be overwhelming, our citizens have reacted in many ways.

Some have questioned whether we should expose our scandals. Some go so far as to suggest that we cover them up so we can give the world a more flattering picture.

Some withdraw into a shell of bitterness and futility, and leave the field clear for the active corruptionists. A few people even decide to join the thieves, after erroneously concluding that you can't beat them.

With no answers of their own, many people have rushed to join groups or societies with programs in which it is contended they have found "the basic problem." These groups are willing to supply what the confused may regard as easy answers. The unknowing find it easier to join without thinking, and end up as supporters of the John Birch Society, the extreme White Citizens groups, the equally extreme Black Muslims, or the Ku Klux Klan.

No amount of warning and reasoning will stop all of the rush of thoughtless citizens who will give their names to extremist groups. A certain amount of this frantic joining can be expected in a free society. However, it is disturbing when groups of college students join the John Birch Society with no real look at all at what this group stands for. It is equally disturbing when large numbers of college students rally to defend the actions of a college professor who has been a party to a "fix" of a television quiz show.

With full knowledge of the corruption in our society, I am still certain that it is relatively clean. I say "relatively clean," for in judging it we must not judge it alone, but we must judge it in comparison with other societies in the world today. With all its weaknesses, it is certainly a better society than that

[69]

of the Communist world where there is no thought of fair play or justice for the individual, and where efforts to hide corruption have only resulted in its festering to the point where it was destroying the production of the farm program.

Certainly we have a better society than that of the Arab world, where the bribing of officials is an ordinary procedure. Certainly it is a more honest society than those found in France or Italy, or in the Far East.

In fact, the argument might be made that our society is so honest in its general operation that it does not know how to grapple with the nearly total corruption in many of the underdeveloped countries where we have foreign aid programs.

If there is anything wrong with our society, it is not because of our system of government. What is wrong is wrong despite our system of government which gives the people of the country the right to insist on high standards, and the mechanism for defeating those who do not strive for honest and efficient government.

If there are things that you don't like, don't be among those who rip at our system and blame our American democracy for everything. It is time for each citizen to look at himself, and to ask himself if he is contributing to the delinquency. He should also ask himself if there isn't something he can do to help eliminate the evils that will inevitably creep into any system.

For the past twenty years, I have had the good fortune to be involved constantly in a study of the problems of government. This work has embraced the entire scale of city, county, state and federal government operations. It has included the exposure of theft and misappropriation of government money. It has included the misuse of government power on local, state and federal levels.

I have seen the side of government operations that does not

flatter our system, and at close range have seen the worst side of hundreds of public officials. Through these twenty years, I believe that I have viewed almost every evil that can creep into our system, but I have not lost faith in that system of government. I know now that I will never lose faith in it.

In nearly every case, our American democracy has forced a reform as soon as the facts had been clearly relayed to the public through the press. Incompetent and corrupt city officials in Des Moines were defeated and the city-manager form of government was adopted. Corrupt and incompetent Polk county officials were indicted, convicted and tossed out of office.

The exposure of corruption in the Truman administration forced wholesale resignations, and there were many indictments and convictions. The revelation of many "conflicts of interest" at high points in the Eisenhower administration resulted in a rash of resignations and a few indictments.

Exposure of the "indiscreet" actions of President Eisenhower's top aide, Mr. Sherman Adams, forced his resignation. I mention Mr. Adams only because he had represented the greatest in White House power, and because events proved that in the American democracy that power could not save him when his relationship with Bernard Goldfine became known to the public.

I have no doubt that present and future administrations will be plagued by similar problems. When the first case of "conflict of interest" or misuse of government funds becomes known we will see a real test of the new administration. Then we will learn how fast it will detect wrongdoing. Then we will learn how quickly the new President is able to put his hands on the true facts, and brush away the excuses and rationalization that always are brought forth to cloud the issue. Then we will learn how effective the President is at driving to the point of the trouble and correcting it.

However, it should not be forgotten that each time there is a test for a President, whether his name is Roosevelt, Truman, Eisenhower or Kennedy, there is a test for you as citizens. If you insist on good government, then you will get government that is relatively clean. If you only follow a political label, whether it is Democratic or Republican, then you are a party to the crimes that are committed, covered up or excused by those elected on your party ticket.

Perhaps some of your neighbors can justify a lack of interest or a lack of knowledge of political issues on grounds that they do not have the background to find their way through complex issues. If you who are college graduates are not informed enough to make balanced judgments on the actions of our political leaders, it is only because you have been too lazy or too irresponsible to learn about the most important institution in your life—our American democracy.

Travel in more than forty countries in the last eleven months has only reinforced my belief in our government, and in the way of life we have found under it. I have reflected on it through the turmoil of Africa, the military tensions of the Middle East, the stern police state in Russia, and the precarious politics of France and many other countries of Western Europe. Freedom is a rare commodity. The totalitarian nationalism sweeping Africa and other underdeveloped areas has been misconstrued as meaning more freedom. It is not so. There are millions in every part of the world who would give all they possess to live here.

I hope that I can make one point stick with you: the American democracy is important, even vital, to the continuation of your opportunities, your freedom and your standard of living. Successful operation of the American democracy is worth all of the work and all of the sacrifice that you can ever make.

We are in the era of the forty-hour week, and there is talk of a thirty-five-hour week in the future with even more "leisure time." The least that any of you should sacrifice is a few hours of your time each week for the reading, study and discussion necessary for you to have a balanced judgment on some of the crucial problems we will face in the next decade. I would stress the term "balanced judgment," for it will be a disservice if you merely join the uninformed chorus as "professional liberals," "professional conservatives," or even as "professional middle-of-the-roaders."

There is a need for liberals who think, and who have the courage to break with the professional liberal views even at the expense of irritating some of their consistently liberal friends.

There is a need for conservatives who will think out problems independently, and are not hemmed in by the thought patterns that are popular with their crowd.

And I can respect a middle-of-the-roader if I feel that he knows why he is in the middle of the road on some issue. He is entitled to no respect if he is simply drifting down the middle because it is the easy, lazy way to drift without making anyone angry.

Unfortunately, our country is plagued with too little thinking on important issues, and too much of the lazy acceptance of the slogans of political parties, government agencies, political figures and advertising agencies.

Unfortunately, too much hero worship and too little thought goes into the selection of our leading political figures. President Eisenhower was elected as a hero of World War II. I will not seek to judge his overall performance, but will leave it to historians with a perspective of many years. However, I will say that President Eisenhower would probably have buckled down to his duties with more vigor and determination if the public had been less adoring and a bit more demanding in the early years of his administration.

President Kennedy was subjected to the same type of public adoration in the first months of his administration. The Cuba affair changed all that, and I am inclined to feel that this sharp slap was a good thing for President Kennedy and for the nation. It jarred President Kennedy with the realization that his performance would not automatically measure up to the standard of his words. It shocked the nation into a realization that our President, our Defense Department and our C.I.A. can make costly miscalculations even on such a relatively small problem as Castro's Cuba.

Cuba will be worth the price if it has awakened the nation, the Kennedy administration and the various departments of government to our weaknesses in such a manner that those weaknesses will be repaired. Cuba will have been in vain if the lessons are forgotten, and if we drift into a state of lethargy. Cuba will be in vain if somehow our government follows a standard pattern of the past—a simple firing or demotion of one man, or a reorganization of a few rules that is given to the public as a substitute for correcting the real weakness.

Our history shows that it takes quite a jolt to shake the public and to force correction of obvious problems in our society.

It took a congressional investigation of major tax scandals in the Truman administration to force President Truman to remove many officials who were engaged in "fixing" tax cases for huge fees. There were revelations of scandalous conditions by Senator John J. Williams, the Delaware Republican, as early as late 1950 and early in 1951. The first speeches by Senator Williams should have aroused the public and forced a major cleaning of the Internal Revenue Service. It took nearly a year of investigations before the public became outraged enough that the Truman administration felt compelled to take drastic action.

Many of you will recall the long months of investigation and prodding that were necessary before the Eisenhower administration took steps to remove certain corrupt officials and to correct the operations of the Federal Communications Commission and other regulatory agencies.

As early as 1953 and 1954, there were some brief congressional hearings on scandals in the Teamsters Union and some other unions. Even then, it was a pattern that was broad enough to demonstrate major corruption in American trade unions—theft of union funds, violence in dispute, abuse of union members, shakedowns of employers, widespread manipulation of union health and welfare funds. There were only a few people concerned about it, and the corrupt trade unions explained it all away as "isolated incidents" that was unrelated to the "basic honesty" of the union movement. It took the McClellan Committee to tell the real story in the 1957–60 period.

It took all the drama of two years of hearings by the McClellan Committee to create a public opinion for legal changes that should have been made five years earlier.

The problem of balance in the labor-management field has not yet been solved. Perfect balance probably never will be achieved. However, there are a number of problems in this area that will be vital in the years ahead. The Teamsters Union represents a tremendous force in our economy. It is a power that is too great for any business to combat. It is an economic power that stretches from coast to coast using its funds for political pressure. It has used this financial power to corrupt local law enforcement, local prosecutors and some federal officials, according to the documented record of the McClellan Committee. Even if the Teamsters Union was not headed by James R. Hoffa and his underworld cronies, it would be an unhealthy arrangement for our nation. Somehow our people and our government officials must find a means to curb this organization with its strangle hold on our transportation. But, on balance, it must be done without any undue interference with the rights of transportation employees to join unions and bargain for better working conditions and wages.

It will require considerable study for you to keep pace with developments in this labor-management area to arrive at balanced conclusions as to what should be done. And control of the Teamsters will be only one of many problems in the union area.

What, if any, limitation should there be on the right to strike? We have been a wealthy enough nation that we have been able to afford the luxury of an unlimited right to strike in our industries. We have been able to afford a lengthy steel strike in 1959, even though it resulted in some of our markets' getting away to foreign competitors. We had a sufficient stock of steel in the United States to take care of most of our pressing needs for steel on defense projects. But, there is a serious question of how long we can afford the luxury of such strikes during a period when we are engaged in a tough competitive struggle against Russia. As you try to answer the questions for yourselves, it will not be enough to parrot the answers of the AFL-CIO or the National Association of Manufacturers.

If this nation is to survive, it will be necessary for a majority of you to do enough thinking to arrive at some kind of a balanced belief of your own on such things. Those of you who are college graduates have had some opportunity to prepare yourselves for thinking independently. If you do not take the time and the trouble to study these problems, then it is unlikely that any large segment of the population will.

New scandals in our military spending have come to light recently. Chairman Edward Hebert, of a House Government Operations subcommittee, has produced his "Chamber of Horrors." The individual examples of waste are bad enough, but the millions wasted are only a symptom of the real trouble: a Defense Department procurement operation that is chronically inefficient, that cannot catch its own errors, and that does virtually nothing to eliminate waste and mismanagement until prodded from Congress or some other outside source.

Our armed services disregarded the legal requirement for bidding on the purchase of spare parts. Officials of the Defense Department certified falsely that there was only one source of supply for hundreds of items to relieve themselves of the responsibility for obtaining bids. The result: they paid as much as three to seven times the price they should have paid for some items. Disregard of the law through collusion or through negligence cost the taxpayers millions of dollars.

This waste was not tied to any political party. To my knowledge, the Congress has been conducting hearings on this subject for ten years. Each year there is a new "Chamber of Horrors" for exhibiting the same pattern of blunders, the same stupidity, and the same negligence. The Truman administration did not stop this blundering and waste. The Eisenhower administration did not stop it, and even gave it an unwitting assist by adopting the broad secrecy of "executive privilege" that allowed Defense Department officials to hide records from Congressional investigators.

The Kennedy administration has no responsibility for certain scandals now revealed, but it does have a responsibility to dig into these cases and eliminate the causes. It will be some time before we are able to judge what, if anything, the Kennedy administration can do to end this wastefulness.

The success in stopping this waste will be in a large measure dependent upon how the citizens of the nation react. If they make their views felt in letters to President Kennedy, in letters to their congressmen and senators and in public forums, then these wrongs will be corrected. If the citizens are unconcerned or cynical or just plain lazy, then it will be more difficult to arouse top officials to follow through in what seems like a disagreeable and thankless task.

Foreign aid is another area to which you will have to give some thoughtful attention in the years ahead. It is laudable for us to favor broad foreign aid programs for humanitarian reasons, or because it is felt that such aid can help establish a healthy economy and the climate for development of free, independent and democratic nations.

However, this does not necessarily mean that it is a mark of statesmanship or good judgment to vote automatically for more and more foreign aid for more and more countries. Balanced belief is not blind belief. A balanced judgment demands that we weigh such programs against our past experiences. And, I might say that in this field we have sufficient experience to know the hazards inherent in loose administration and unwise planning.

There is a serious question about the wisdom of programs when the administrations of those humanitarian programs misfire as they did in Peru. Out of the thirteen million dollars given to Peru for "drought relief," only five per cent actually was given to the drought victims. Another thirty to thirty-five per cent was sold to the drought victims with considerable "profiteering" involved. According to government auditors, about sixty per cent of the funds and goods went into "unauthorized channels."

The result could hardly be regarded as a great triumph for our program of federal aid. It could hardly be argued in this case that our humanitarian motives would be repaid with a warm gratitude. In fact, it could be argued that the United States drought relief program in Peru merely gave some Peruvian officials an opportunity for making huge profits from the misery of their countrymen. This was not our object in giving.

Our experiences in Laos, Turkey and Iran have been little better than in Peru. Laos aid was the source of dozens of major scandals that were covered up for years by the International Cooperation Administration. Instead of the fine roads, economic development and social reform that were expected, there was large-scale profiteering for a privileged class. There was corruption and mismanagement that involved some United States officials and former United States officials. Now Laos is going down the drain.

The mismanagement and corruption in our foreign aid programs in Turkey and Iran have been apparent to everyone. A military *coup d'état* upset the corrupt Menderes regime in Turkey in June, 1960. Iran is reported in financial ruin despite oil resources and millions in U.S. aid. Iran is still a scene of discontent, and this nation could end up in a full-scale revolution at any time.

In none of these cases has U.S. aid resulted in establishing a healthy economy, even though it could always be argued that the economic condition in each would be worse without our aid. Certainly it would not be possible to class Laos, Turkey and Iran as being "free, independent and democratic nations."

Balanced belief requires the active interest in our foreign

aid programs so you will know what programs are failures and which are successful. Balanced belief requires that you have enough information to understand that all who voted for unrestricted foreign aid are not necessarily on the side of the angels. It requires the ability to see that all who try to limit or restrict such programs are not necessarily villains with an isolation complex.

All of us favor a fair trial for all persons accused of crime, and most of us believe that this should include all safeguards of basic constitutional rights. But, unless we have a balanced belief on this subject, it is easy for us to be misled by defense lawyers who are only interested in springing their underworld clients. And the misleading can also be accomplished by political judges who are warping "fair trial" guarantees to take care of a friend or to follow out some personal political ideology.

In the maze of hair-splitting decisions and well-planned confusion, the public often loses sight of the basic purpose of a trial—the simple purpose of finding the truth without exerting coercion on witnesses or defendants. It is often forgotten that there is also a right of society to be protected from criminals. It is often forgotten that society is entitled to administration of our laws and our courts so there is reasonable assurance that those guilty of crime will be punished.

Honest law enforcement is vital to the continued success of our American democracy. The enemy within—the organized criminals—are just as real a threat to our nation as the thrusts of the Communist world.

You have been shocked at the television stories of the "Untouchables" of the nineteen twenties. Yet, most of you should be aware that we have our "untouchables" today who are even more powerful. In the nineteen twenties they had control in a few cities; now they operate from coast to coast.

They have more money, and often they are operating behind such façades as the labor unions.

If they are allowed to continue, they can destroy our government from within. It is your obligation and your responsibility to avoid any activity that aids their cause. It is not only right but wise to avoid any entanglements with this group in the early stages of your career, for it could make you a captive for life.

Today we are a nation with as many problems as at any point in our history. I have pointed to only a few of these major problems in hopes that some of you will see the opportunity that exists in these areas.

I am reminded of the comment of Baron Rothschild, who said, "For me there are no good times or bad times; every time is an opportunity."

In addition to informing yourselves generally about your government, each of you has the ability to delve deeply into one of these major problem areas to make a significant contribution to your community and to yourself. Don't wait for four or five years to try your hand at understanding and solving some major problems. Move into it immediately. Remember that Jefferson and Hamilton were young men when they were key figures in government. I even hear reports that there are a few young men in Washington in some top offices today.

When I have stressed a "balanced belief," it has not been an effort to get you to memorize the encyclopedia or even the Code of Iowa. To come to grips with the rights or wrongs on a specific case can often be relatively simple if you enter the search with an open mind, insist on facts rather than any emotion in determining your stand, and constantly question your position.

And, above all, don't be concerned if once in a while you are out of step with the thinking of your friends. There is much more to be concerned about if you are too much in agreement with your friends on all issues—too much inclined to line up as total liberal or total conservative. Don't be a cynic. Don't be lazy. Don't be fainthearted about the future of our American democracy. It can continue as the best system of government the world has known if you are willing to do your part. Remember, "Every time is an opportunity" if you are an independent with a balanced belief. There is no opportunity in being just one of the sheep.

CLARK R. MOLLENHOFF, lawyer and journalist, has won many awards for skilled writing, including the Clapper Award and the Pulitzer Prize (1958).

EDUCATION AND DEMOCRACY

Conrad A. Elvehjem

THE complexity of our society, and of the university which is society's microcosm, has made it extremely difficult for any but the brave and the wise to exploit the strength of their personal freedom to its fullest usefulness. Despite high ideals and great ambitions, it is easier to let someone else do it. In the case of the university, it then becomes the legislature, the regents, the president and deans, but mostly the faculty, who must somehow get most students to learn and to exercise that greatest student freedom—the right to use their minds.

I would like to teach in a university in which there were no rules or regulations, no assignments or examinations—only students so eager to learn that those prods to learning would be unnecessary. For those of you continuing in graduate school, there is a measure of this ahead for you. For those of you leaving formal education—the university without rules is yours. Your freedom now to learn is absolute. Make sure you do as well without examinations as you have done with them.

There is no immorality in state support of education, no restriction of freedom tied to such support, so long as scholars demand and use their freedom. Quite the opposite—state support, which is in reality the support of all the citizens, can guarantee academic freedom against the intrusion of special interest groups. But to maintain such freedom, all the people must know its value, and thus education itself becomes fundamental to freedom. It is because our forefathers saw this link between education and freedom that schools and colleges were given early priority in the development of our young nation.

"By far the most important bill in our whole code," Thomas Jefferson wrote, "is that for the diffusion of knowledge among the people. No other sure foundation can be devised for the preservation of freedom and happiness . . . the tax which will be paid for this purpose is not more than the thousandth part of what will be paid . . . if we leave the people in ignorance."

Today, when international competition has brought new attention to education as a force for progress, it is well to recall that it has been, first, a force for freedom. In our drive to use education as a tool for military defense we should not hinder its use as a tool for building better people, free people.

To the individual, to the state and to our hopes for world peace, it is more important to extend man's freedom than his flight through space. But these things are not at cross purposes. True, a man whose freedom allows him to study what interests him may not produce just what the people may desire at that moment, but left to follow his own path he is a thousand times more likely to produce significant progress than if he were shackled to an assigned task. This is freedom's strength.

The emerging peoples of the underdeveloped nations are rising in a world divided into two great camps. They find themselves caught in the crossfire of ideologies—the free world pitted against the unfree—and discover themselves to be the prizes in this critical contest. Although they have some voice in who shall win, from their limited viewpoint, the choice that must be made is unclear.

They have four very basic needs: food, shelter, education and recognition. The materialistic world that greets them on both sides offers as inducements, from each point of view, help with food and shelter and other matters economic, but little help with sustenance for the mind and spirit—education and individual recognition.

True, both the free world and the soviet have made halting efforts to meet these needs of the spirit and the mind, but in nothing like the measure that is required for their satisfaction. Our own nation is broadening, to some extent, its educational exchanges, and implements them with the Peace Corps. But at best, these are halfhearted efforts, considering the magnitude of the need.

There are at least two important advantages in providing educational aid. First, it enables the people aided to help themselves; and second, it provides individual recognition—symbolizes our belief in human dignity—in most dramatic terms.

Education, made widely available and applied to human needs through the Land Grant tradition, did much to make ours the rich, independent and free nation it is today. Our present universities—our states—could never have reached their present levels if, a century ago, Abraham Lincoln had not signed that visionary document, the Land Grant Act, which gave federal impetus to higher education throughout our nation. If we, today, had the vision and the faith in education that our pioneering leaders possessed, we would extend the idea that meant so much to our nation's progress to the far reaches of the world.

It is not reckless to say that such a move, if taken boldly, ambitiously and soon, could change the course of history— ultimately could build the world-wide peace and prosperity that all men of good will so earnestly seek. But to make such a telling move requires faith in education far beyond that we have thus far shown. It calls for exploitation to the fullest of the power of education.

Let us turn the tractors into books, the dams into schoolhouses, the military specialists into teachers. Let us concentrate on the things of the mind and the spirit, not material aid.

Granted, hunger must be satisfied, man must be shielded from the elements. But given widespread education, he can meet these needs himself—and he would rather, for human dignity is not enhanced by the dole.

Education for peace is my charge. I know it can be done.

CONRAD A. ELVEHJEM died on July 27, 1962, shortly after this book went into preparation. He was President of the University of Wisconsin, a native son of that state, and the recipient of innumerable honors and distinctions, academic and otherwise. It is hoped that his speech will remain as some testament to his most useful life and his love for American education.

THE FREE SOCIETY

Rufus C. Harris

THE free society, said Pericles of the Golden Age of Athens, is one where the majority rules, yet minority rights are well respected; it is one where prestige, opportunity and leadership are founded on established merit; where public decisions are made after uninhibited public discussion; where tolerance of individual differences in private life prevails; where neighbor does not impose his anger upon neighbor when he does not agree with him. It is not surprising that among the many legacies which we have from the Greeks free inquiry was the most precious, because free personal action was their ardent desire. Pluralism in religion, experimentation in government, indulgence of adverse opinion and fearless sifting of ideas dominated their culture. From their early pioneering days down to the conquest of Alexander the Great, there was incessant praise of the courageous venture of the human mind.

That Golden Age, however, like all such ages, passed on. Radical change occurred in Athenian social action. Initiative and responsibility gradually yielded to political and religious authority; confidence in the rational direction of individual experience and social institutions was lost.

What brought this about? It resulted chiefly, I suspect, from an unconscious flight from the heavy burden of individual choice which a free society always lays upon its members. Urban life became so complex and the range of knowledge so great that people retreated first from the attempt to understand, and later from the effort to control their lives rationally. It became easier to cast their burdens on the high priests or on leaders who were anxious to accept the responsibility—and the power! Escapism became the order of the time—escape into the specialized professions, into social clubs, into artistic circles, into mystic cults, and even into the homes, in deep apathy. The citizens finally became conformists, and on the great issues of their common life they found it easier and safer to have no opinion. The Golden Age was lost.

There is obvious danger in drawing historical analogies and in oversimplifying complex situations. Yet I suggest that in countless ways our present twentieth century life may be similar to that condition. We now live in a world with a vast range of complexities. Our time may well be more difficult than that of any other period. The temptation, consequently, toward conformity is unobtrusively overpowering. In such a period of confusion, uncertainty and frustration, it is not difficult to accept leadership which promises facile, untroublesome and quick answers. With so many beguiling voices urging us to shape our lives by their patterns and to take our directions from them, a unique psychological urge is stirred within us to abandon our individual free judgments and personal responsibilities.

This impulse is strengthened by several incidents in our national background. One is the recurring harsh treatment which free thought encountered in our amazing national development. Suspicion and distrust of intellectuals were notable elements in several stages of our pioneering experience. On every frontier there were some leaders, and some ordinary settlers, who were hostile to higher education. During the eighteenth century, and later, there was extensive criticism of professional men. The nineteenth century admired the "know-nothings." During our time we have observed and encouraged scorn and suspicion of learning by labeling learned men "brain trusters" and "eggheads." Concrete for roads and steel for bridges gain the approval of executives and legislators more readily than teacher pay and school improvement. An unlovely strain in our national heritage contains both a distrust of intellectual activity and a refusal to recognize the moral obligation to respect intelligence.

Our predicament is complicated additionally by a new appraisal of the limitations of the mind on human conduct. Many intellectuals now may be described as somewhat anti-intellectual in the sense that psychological discoveries have made them realize that forces other than rational ones dictate so much of human conduct; that human beings are moved by complicated emotional drives, habits, and conditioned reflexes which the mind with infinite patience can understand to some extent but which it cannot govern. There has arisen, consequently, a new pessimism, ironic among intellectuals who yearn to hold that philosophy or reason is the pilot of private endeavor and social action.

A further deterrent to our free enterprise of the mind is a somewhat doltish passion for standardization. Everything must be standardized—mind as well as matter! This standardization has been aided by tremendous progress in technology and in the means of communication. We must, of course justify in terms of efficiency our standardized gadgets, but what shall we say about standardized information and standardized ideas? Who, if anyone, for instance, controls our newspapers? It has been asserted that too many of them represent chiefly one political and economic philosophy; that we have, by and large, a one-party and one-philosophy press; that many of our cities have but one slant on the news since a large number of them have no competing publishing plants.

Who, in a fashion, if anyone, controls our education? School board members and trustees for the most part are businessmen and lawyers. Although there is no question about their ability, nor any about their devotion to education and to the general welfare, it has been suggested that they cherish one economic point of view and represent one social level. Who, if anyone, controls our motion pictures and our radio and television programs? It is heard that a few large business firms can employ or discharge script writers almost at will. Who controls our state governments? In about twenty states, several of them Democratic and several Republican, there exists a virtual political monopoly, with one party rather consistently holding most of the state offices and the seats in the legislatures. Conditions such as these add up to a situation which invites, if it does not urge, conformity. A free society needs the constant interplay and challenge of information, ideas, suggestions, differences, criticisms and evaluations. But this diversity thus becomes difficult to obtain, and Arnold Toynbee describes its lack as one which is opposite to the differentiation and competition which mark the growth stage of civilization.

In the cold war the suppression of ideas reaches even more serious proportions. Apprehension stemming from our new role of world leadership; awareness of the difficulty of our task; cognizance of our poor preparation to handle our commitments; concern over the continuing menace of communism—these have enabled some groups and individuals to exploit the national anxieties to serve a misguided patriotism by organizing what may be called superpatriotic societies. One such, I suspect, is the John Birch Society, which assumed the name of a Mercer graduate of the Class of 1939—the name of a conscientious, dedicated, and probably immature young man, long dead and unable to consent to the employment of his name. Such groups on both sides—right and left—by reckless and exaggerated charges readily smear their fellow citizens for holding contrary points of view. In the role of Procrustes, extremists have sought to force conformity to their patterns. They do not seem to respect, not to mention comprehend, our historic American principles of civil rights contained in the first ten amendments to the Constitution, which were adopted almost along with it. They have abused some proven and revered leaders, and have cast suspicion on public officials and national policies. Consequently, many persons and institutions have become afraid to voice unpopular opinions, or indeed opinions of any kind. Is it any surprise that university students are becoming unwilling to commit themselves on a variety of social issues for fear of future reprisals? It may be doubted that a country so powerful and protected as this has ever been subjected to such internal assaults of irrational fears, suspicions and accusations, or compelled to allow so many intellectual lights to be extinguished.

Why do I recite these matters to you? It is because I believe that the essence of the free society is threatened by such limitations on individual action, thought and expression, and by the subsequent suspension of choice and judgment of ideas; and that college graduates should combat such limitations. Our public policy cannot be determined wisely without the adequate consideration of various alternatives. Insistence on conformity is burdensome, if not deadly, to our advancement.

In his address several years ago, the president of the Association for the Advancement of Science drew an interesting physiological analogy to the body politic. He said that in a healthy human body myriads of differentiated cells are organized into functional, cooperating organs. Any form of dictatorship by an individual organ results in degeneration or death. "Tyranny in the body is best illustrated," he said, "by a cancer. Its action eventually destroys the organism." So in a healthy society. Many individuals and groups must make contributions to the welfare of the whole, and if any individual or group acquires domination the entire social organism may be destroyed. Intelligent and tested variety is a requisite of social health.

All of the contemporary, boundless, constrictive distortions of the processes of our free society are symptomatic of something. They are symptomatic of an unhealthy and dangerous state of mind. They are unhealthy because they are abnormal to freedom. They are dangerous because they endanger our self-respect and happiness. "The secret of happiness," said Pericles, "is freedom, and freedom is created by courage. Unless there is an open market for ideas and an opportunity for people to engage in the free enterprise of the mind and voice their convictions, men will fall short," he said, "of enjoying full citizenship in the republic of free human values."

Education has a vital role and an apt place in the present state of our need because the free society must have steady development of free men. The essential problem in this development is the favorable conduct and character of American life as a whole. Much more is at issue here than the matter of schooling, vital as it is to all citizens, white and black. The chief matter at issue is whether the people will allow the democratic aspiration adequate opportunity to survive and to flourish. If we anticipate that education can readily or quickly assure this, we will be mistaken. Education itself will do well to survive the present threats, for it is not swift-moving and cannot engage in its transforming job on short schedule. It is directed at those who are precisely what the word "immature" suggests: undeveloped, helpless, dependent. Its chief impact on a society is through the individual, and the individual requires time and support—props! The effective use of that time is such occasions as graduation, which is a recognition of the prized "transformation" of a band of young citizens. Such "transformation" is no easy achievement because while the school has the student, that student at the same time is "had," so to speak, by all the rest of his culture. Family, church, club, highway, sand lot, screen, television, radio and comic book—all are competitive forces of large potency. They reduce the school for many individuals to the uninspiring status of lesson-giver and lesson-bearer.

The schools have no monopoly on the minds of those they instruct, and often they have no hold on their loyalties. While no miracle can speed their processes to make them amenable to crash performance, it is hugely important that the people believe their fruits are good, even as they believe that their processes are sometimes misdirected. Such faith is justified by the testimony of history, which asserts that though the world may blow up while its improvement is sought, yet such risk must be assumed, and it reveals in countless ways that educational endeavor may produce, even though slowly, the solid foundation for our advancement.

Although the faith to which we are entitled is not ungrounded, we must ever furrow the ground anew. This is the essential task of Christian education. The transformed, mature and effective architects of the good society which we seek will not come forth merely because we wish for them or because we open, or keep open, the school doors to all the children of all the people. More is necessary. Maturity in Christian understanding and purpose is needed. These aims should be included in the prized "development" of those who will serve most effectively to free society and its processes. A major aspect of this service is a heightened appreciation of the Christian heritage and promise. By their acceptance and benediction we are offered the hope that we may find the noble social establishments and ways that pledge no absence of problems and contradictions in our future, but provide the wise approaches to them which will lead to their effective resolution.

RUFUS C. HARRIS, President of Mercer University, Macon, Georgia, has been a lawyer, a professor of law and a college administrator.

A LOOK AT ACADEMIC FREEDOM

Louis H. Heilbron

ACADEMIC freedom is an ancient heritage and has been variously defined. According to one authority, it is principally designed "to protect the teacher from hazards that tend to prevent him from meeting his obligation in the pursuit of truth." According to another, it "is the assertion that scholars, teacher and student both, shall have the freedom to study, teach, publish and discuss that which they themselves consider to be appropriate to the field of their competence or study; it exists only if these rights can be exercised without fear of punitive actions that will affect the present or future welfare of the scholar." It has also been said "that the freedoms of the scholar are simply the freedoms of thought and speech which all individuals claim, and that the scholar has no special rights that are not given to other citizens." But the term as commonly used does imply certain rights and

[95]

obligations peculiar to the university or college atmosphere. It is worth underlining that academic freedom relates to the pursuit of truth, and not necessarily to its capture. Thus the conscientious teachers in the thirteenth century who may have taught that the earth is stationary in the center of the universe were probably discharging their teaching responsibilities just as were those who taught biology before Darwin and those who taught physics before Einstein. The borders of knowledge limit the expression of academic freedom. And who today knows for certain which of the many economic theories explaining the cause and cure of the economic cycle is the true one? So it is in the *quest* for truth that the important freedom of the scholar lies.

This whole concept has a considerable history which at this time we can only touch upon. But it is important to pause a moment and refer to two factors from the past which give color and meaning to our subject. One rests in the origin of the university or college as we know it; the other in the philosophy of eighteenth century thought as exemplified by the utterances of the founding fathers of our Constitution and form of government.

Our institutions of higher education are the direct descendants of the medieval European university. The very structure, ritual and nomenclature of a modern college has medieval roots. It is true that some of the titles had a little different meaning than they have today. For example, "Master," "Doctor," and "Professor" in a medieval university described the same person, and the terms "Chancellor" and "Regent" had a different connotation, but most of the old terms are still used in one form or another. For better or for worse, the idea of exacting oaths from teachers and students has come down to us from these early days. In the Middle Ages a supplicant for a degree had to swear that he attended the university lectures; when he was a candidate for an examination he had to swear that he would not offer a bribe to the examiner and the examiner had to swear that he would not receive one. Moreover, the candidate in some universities swore that he would not wreak his vengeance by knife or dagger upon an examiner who failed him. The obedience to almost every university regulation was enforced by an oath. The whole system was predicated on penalties for perjury, involving spiritual penalties in this life and in the life hereafter. Subsequently, it was found that the fine of a half crown proved to be a better deterrent and was adopted.

The most important aspect of the medieval university was its independence: it had its own guild or corporate structure and was self-governing. In some places it was more independent of the Church than in others, but in all cases it evidenced its ecclesiastical origins. (The independent church orders also had considerable freedom to operate their own affairs.) Actually, a medieval university such as Oxford was a unit of government. If its scholars became involved, as they did, in tavern brawls in the town, and someone was injured or killed in the struggle, the medieval university exercised criminal jurisdiction and decided the cases. Indeed, when the townspeople of Oxford caused a number of fatalities among the Oxford scholars, the University (besides invoking other penalties) imposed an annual fine and penance "in perpetuity" on the municipal authorities and it was not until 1829, after the passage of almost five hundred years, that the mayor of Oxford ceased to come to a University chapel with his hat in hand, meekly to do penance and apologize for an incident that occurred in 1354! Actually, Oxford was a small town away from the main currents of political and social life and the masters and scholars ordinarily pursued their studies in their own way and under their own rules, free from the interference of king or bishop. Still, isolation was not necessary to the security of the medieval university. One of the greatest of the medieval universities was that of Paris, called "the elder daughter of the King." The governmental administration of France was quite dependent upon selecting its advisors and administrators from the students trained and developed in that university. And the King gave a special protection to the University; even in the bitter wars between England and France, the English students attending the University of Paris were fully protected. Even the all-powerful Inquisition was held back by the intellectual ramparts of this great institution and its cruel instruments were blunted in Northern France.

Thus the medieval university in its corporate capacity had special rights and privileges. It was in its own way a sanctuary. The scholar within its walls had the freedom to study, to discuss and to argue, and often when he ventured beyond its walls the long arm of the university stretched out to shield him. Grants from the sovereign or from the Church, fees collected from the scholars, chests or endowments to which the public made contributions, all supported the finances of the university. These institutions were small islands of light in a dark sea of illiteracy. Their members were privileged, and constituted an elite. They were citadels of the intellect, strong, independent and respected.

I do not mean to suggest that these very early universities were superior to modern institutions; naturally their curriculum was restricted to the confines of knowledge and thought then available; much of what they taught is now disproved or discredited. But their independent structure is the source of the special claim of academic freedom today.

As I have previously indicated, there is a second historical experience that bears upon our subject. In the latter part of the eighteenth century along the Atlantic seaboard of the Thirteen Colonies there existed a body of men of extraordinary breadth and stature, especially in their understanding of the theory and the art of government. They had inherited the best of the English tradition concerning individual freedoms; indeed they were its guardians at a time when the mother country was neglecting them. They were learned in the French writings and the aspirations expressed in them for political and social freedom, and they were responsible for our Declaration of Independence, our Constitution and appended Bill of Rights. They reached their final decisions on the Constitution after undergoing the experience of an inadequate system of government under the Articles of Confederation and after much debate, controversy and compromise. The most relevant point which we can mention about their deliberations and their expressions is that they were the work of reasonable men. The eighteenth century is titled the Age of Reason. The Federalist Papers which were designed to persuade the people of the sovereign states to support the adoption of the Federal Constitution of the United States are masterpieces of persuasion and of reason. This was not the forum for the hot-tempered, the extremist, the demagogue. These men fought hard for their views and they won— with *reason*. And one of their victories was the First Amendment.

In these days when controversies occur concerning the application of our constitutional rights and privileges, they are sometimes urged in a spirit of heat and hysteria which would not be understandable to those who wrote our basic documents. It may well be that there are occasions when our freedom to think, to believe and to express must be asserted in strong and passionate terms and it is true that the rule of reason is not written into the Constitution to control what we think and how we express it. Nevertheless, of all places where we might expect that the exercise of these rights would reflect their eighteenth century enlightened American origin, where we might expect more light than heat, it is on the college campus. This is where we should find, in discussions pro and con, the greatest degree of objectivity on the part of faculty and students; this is where we should find the most evident desire to have fair play for all competing points of view and to have them properly analyzed and represented.

Now the modern universities and colleges, both public and private, have lost some of the administrative privileges which distinguished the university guild or public corporation of the Middle Ages. But there lingers in their tradition the idea of a special sanctuary. We continue to believe that of all places on earth the college campus should be the most protected area for free discussion and comparison of ideas, the busiest market place for the exchange of knowledge, the farthest frontier from which most adventures into learning may be undertaken. In this favorable climate academic freedom should flourish, and with it the larger right of freedom of speech. Indeed there is an interrelationship between the two: The scholar should always speak as a reasonable man inside or outside the "sanctuary." The scholar's claim of academic freedom carries with it its own particular obligations.

May I enlarge upon this statement by suggesting certain principles which might cover the modern college faculty (later I will deal with the students) in the exercise of their freedoms and responsibilities:

1. Academic freedom is assured to a scholar who meets his obligation to be honest in his work. He makes his presentation in the classroom after having made diligent inquiry and research; his goal is that of impartiality and objectivity and he is prepared to accept or

revise the conclusions and evaluations which are dictated by his work. It is essential to the survival of our society that this freedom, so exercised, be zealously protected by all of us.

It does not follow that a scholar need always be completely neutral in giving his evaluations or conclusions. However, it is important that he indicate such bias as he may have, and that he recognize and give full attention and emphasis to different or opposing positions.

But if a faculty member has an overriding loyalty contrary to the scholarship standards which I have described, if his conclusions and evaluations are dictated by dogma of the totalitarian left, and I refer to that of the Communist Party, or of the totalitarian right, he will have forfeited his right to the protection of that academic freedom which he seeks to dishonor or to destroy. Indeed, he has no place on the faculty.

2. If the faculty member uses the authority of his academic position to win the support of his students for his own political or social points of view in public controversial matters, the right of academic freedom is abused. In other words, he has the responsibility to refrain from indoctrinating his students. He still retains his right to participate as a citizen in political activity and, what is more, he can encourage students as citizens to participate in such activity in accordance with their preferences.

3. If the faculty member addresses the general public on a pending public issue, he is speaking as a citizen but still has special obligations imposed by his position. In the words of the American Association of University Professors which were viewed favorably by the State Board of Education:

As a man of learning and an educational officer, he should remember that the public may judge his profession and his institution by his utterances. Hence he should at all times be accurate, should exercise appropriate restraint, should show respect for the opinions of others, and should make every effort to indicate that he is not an institutional spokesman.

Admittedly it is sometimes difficult for a faculty member to effect complete disassociation from his college. The purpose of the disassociation is, of course, to show that his opinion on a public issue is his own and that he is not using his association to obtain a hearing or to make his point. A good test as to whether he is using the institution as an instrument for the promulgation of ideas which otherwise might not obtain an audience is to ask, Would this statement of views be of interest without indicating it came from Professor Jones of Calford College?

4. If the faculty member enters into the arena of public controversy, he can expect that his views will encounter objections and criticism just as in the case of any other citizen. The college association will confer no immunity against counterattack, but his right, as described, to speak as a citizen should not affect his status as a faculty member.

5. When the faculty member acts in accord with the principles of academic freedom, he is assured against any reprisals that would affect his welfare as a scholar. If disciplinary or punitive action is attempted, he should protect his position by following the orderly procedures of investigation and appeal set up within each college, and if the problem remains, by following the appropriate

state procedure of appeal or review, and not attempt to try his case in advance by newspaper, demonstration or other device of public clamor, which is contrary to the dignity and tradition of his profession.

What about the students? In medieval times the students were considered to be scholars along with their masters and entitled to many of the same privileges. Learning freedom is a natural corollary to teaching freedom, and certainly applies to our colleges of today. The student's freedom to learn is as broad as his professor's freedom to teach.

The current issue is the manner and extent of student participation in the area of public controversial questions. On this matter the experience of the medieval university offers few parallels. Students were always involved in some controversy with a town official in the early days. The Middle Ages were violent times, and students often carried their bows and arrows and used them in the streets. These students were a hardy lot, although some were little more than fourteen years of age; they had traveled long distances over primitive roads and braved the attacks of highwaymen merely to join the university; and they insisted on full tankards of ale and would have shot a tavern keeper who demanded an ID card.

Times have changed and with it the relations between Town and Gown. The Gown lives according to the rules of the Town, and not vice versa.

For a great many years the attitude of the American student toward public issues has been one of apathy and indifference. He has poured his energies into the extracurricular activities of the campus, into intramural and extramural athletic competitions and contests and into the self-government of the student body. Only in the area of the student press has there been a real sensitivity to freedom of expression; as soon as a student becomes editor of his college newspaper he tends to feel the power, if not the restraint, of a Walter Lippmann and he proceeds to declare his views for the benefit of the student body and society. There is a certain exuberance in college newspapers that is refreshing, and in general, I think, they have established a very good record.

This situation is beginning to change, as you know. How should we regard this change? Before answering the question it may be of interest to compare student activities in Europe and in Latin America. There has been a tradition in European universities, especially on the Continent, to participate directly in affairs of state. The sixteen demands of the ill-fated Hungarian revolution were formulated by a student union. Students in France and Italy have manned the barricades and joined in demonstrations and strikes. In the few universities in Africa modeled after European universities, the students are actively engaged in movements for social and political reform. (This is bound to be the case where the vast masses of a country are illiterate and where the natural leadership will come from the privileged few who are in attendance in the halls of higher learning.)

Perhaps the greatest and most influential activity among students is shown in Latin American institutions of higher learning. There, students have been in the vanguard of revolution and reform. In some of the Latin American countries the students participate in the councils which employ the faculty. If they don't like the way a faculty member teaches, or what he teaches, out he goes. In more than one instance, if the students did not like an examination, they have struck and walked out on it.

I would not be surprised if some of you would have liked to have walked out on certain of your examinations or to have struck against some direction to prepare a term paper by a given date. And it may be that you would have welcomed the opportunity to have shared in the employment of your own instructors. It might be pleasant to speculate upon these possibilities. The truth is that student control over faculty does not help the cause of academic freedom or of truth. A faculty which cowers before its students has lost its freedom and its authority.

American student expression on public issues is developing in these particulars:

1. There are many student forums on campus in which the issues of the day are presented by public figures who are subjected to the cross-examination of free student inquiry.

2. The major political parties have established student clubs on many campuses; this is in line with citizenship responsibilities.

3. There have been a number of demonstrations over various issues ranging from disarmament to Congressional inquiry to capital punishment. Such demonstrations are supported by the right of assembly. On the whole, however, the American student does not like to carry banners or to march under slogans or to engage in mass demonstrations.

Now I would not, if I could, try to stop the awakening interest of American students in the political and social and international issues of the day. I think it is an extremely healthy development. This is a tense and serious world in which we live, and the question of survival is the most important of them all. It is right and proper that the students of our colleges should recognize and consider these vital issues. You are called upon sooner or later to serve in our military forces, you may be candidates for the Peace Corps; the world may not be your oyster, but it is at least your prickly pear, and you may want to stick a fork into it.

If you do—and when I say "you" I am referring to college students generally—I suggest that the following principles might govern student expression:

1. Student forums should not be one-sided but should present varying or opposing viewpoints upon controversial issues by competent and responsible authorities. (This does not mean that all points of view have equal validity.)

2. Group student expression should be an expression emanating *from* the campus and not be an expression or demonstration directed and manipulated from the outside.

3. While students cannot be held to the same background of scholarship or objectivity as the faculty, they should recognize that what they do and say—and how they say and do it (in good taste or in bad)—will be considered by the public as indicative of the kind of education they are receiving at the institution they attend.

4. When students express themselves as citizens they should not use the name or the identification of the college; they should make it clear that they are speaking or acting on their own.

5. It should not be expected in a country such as ours, where government is stable and literacy is high, that student political activity would be effective in the same way or would take the same form as in countries where these conditions do not obtain.

Naturally, the trustees of the state colleges are concerned with the protection of academic freedom in the state colleges, and with the general right of freedom of expression. We are just as concerned with the responsibilities that go hand in hand with these freedoms. We are prepared to do our share to defend these freedoms and to protect against their abuse.

In the last analysis, however, the exercise of academic freedom and related responsibilities does not begin with the Legislature, or the governor, or the trustees, or the chancellor. These are matters which are the direct concern of each of the colleges—its faculty (especially the new Senate or Council formed, or in the process of formation, in all of the state colleges), administration and students.

Be conscious of these important rights and responsibilities. Support your college in their proper exercise. Apply the principle of reasonableness in making your own decisions on public issues—when you vote, when you determine to join or not to join one group or another, when you urge some course for the civic welfare. Read your newspaper, listen to your radio, watch your TV—critically. Exhibit that amiable skepticism that has made Missouri a famous state. Don't be fenced in by your own or anyone else's preconceived notions. Form your opinions after the facts, not before. Just be a decent, fair-minded human being—willing to listen and to look, to read and to examine before you act—and you will have justified your college education and all the ancient traditions of academic freedom. What is more, you will be the kind of citizen we need most.

Louis H. Heilbron, attorney, is chairman of the State College System of California. During World War II he was on the Board of Economic Warfare and was also an officer in Europe. His principal interest, apart from his profession, lies in improving American education.

FREEDOM AND WAR

Robert W. Burns

THE years from 1945 to now can well be termed the period
of the greatest technological progress the world has known.
Already atomic energy, jet aircraft, and polio vaccine are
commonplace and not significantly newsworthy. More recently, man's efforts to explore outer space have captured
the headlines, and the prospects for success are so real that
we now wonder why we considered the Buck Rogers comic
strip a fantasy.

But I must also remind you of other headlines. Think
about Laos, Cuba, the Congo, Algeria—and don't forget
Montgomery, lest we think the troubles all belong to somebody else. The point to be made here is that while we have
chalked up signal successes, we have also recorded some dis-
mal failures. To me, the simple truth is that while our scientific community has accepted the challenge of the age, our

political and sociological world has not. It is indeed para-doxical that the success of science has at the same time created or aggravated, or made more intense, political prob-lems. Man simply has not demonstrated an ability to live with his fellows in peace and harmony. Now you can quickly point out to me that this problem has been with us since the beginning of time. You can remind me that Cain and Abel had troubles, too. And you may wonder what's different about this year that makes the problem especially acute. I think these are some of the major differences:

First, the world has a greater density of population than ever before, and the trend is toward an ever-increasing rate. Some observers have called it a population explosion. The fact is that those areas of our globe best suited for human habitation are getting crowded.

Next to be considered is our fairly recent ability to bring more and more people into contact with each other. No spot on the globe is now more than a few hours away. Individual and national interests are impinging on each other as never before.

And certainly not to be omitted from this list is the fact that mankind now has the capability to threaten seriously, if not destroy, human life on this earth.

We have been aware that all was not right with the world, but we have tended to look on those most vocal in their con-cern as eggheads or idealists—to paraphrase C. P. Snow, "Something like a cave man before arithmetic had been in-vented, sneering at those who had the knack of counting on their fingers." An attitude hardly conducive to attracting the effort really needed. But it is now apparent to me that there is a stark necessity to get the situation under control.

Not surprisingly, the most obvious area of conflicting in-terests and ideology today is that between Communism and democracy, two political systems poles apart. Now I don't propose to use this forum to enlarge on this subject. I am certain that all of you are aware of this challenge to our religious principles, our political and economic systems, and our very lives. No doubt you recognize that this particular struggle has the center of the stage because of the relative power positions of the two contestants. But the same struggle is going on in other areas, and while lacking the urgency of this big one, is no less intense. I suspect that these so-called small problems or minor irritants also need prime consideration.

Now I don't profess to be an expert in human relations or politics. I have trouble maintaining the peace in my own household. But I have made some observations that I believe are pertinent. Our Western democratic system is dedicated to the proposition that man must determine for himself how he will be governed. By being governed, I intend to suggest that whole gamut of relationships that each man has for his family, his neighbor, his country and the world. If human life exists on other planets, then this, too, must enter the equation. While we cherish human freedom, I am afraid we fail to be equally aware of the essential restraints on human freedom. Man is a gregarious animal and tends to think of his own interests as paramount. In reality, Robinson Crusoe was the only really free man, and he lost quite a bit of it when Friday came along. In this country our solution has been the evolution of a system of law designed to promote the maximum of freedom without infringement. This system of law represents our recognition of the requirement for man to surrender some of his individual freedom for the common good. This legal code and judicial system doesn't always produce results satisfactory to us all. But I hope we have recognized that, imperfect as it is, the preservation and perfecting of the system is essential to the welfare of us all.

In the international sphere I see a great void in this respect. The only example that comes to mind of man regulating himself in extranational affairs is in the world of commerce. Here, economic interests obviously outweigh other considerations. It is no surprise that the system works well because the participants want it to work—in fact, know that it has to work, if international trade is to continue. But why aren't we equally concerned about the more abstract areas? I suspect it's because until recently the necessity wasn't apparent. But look at the price we are paying for this neglect. The nuclear test ban talks have been going on in Geneva for over three years and the prospects for success are not encouraging. The U.N. can't maintain authority in the Congo. There has been a war going in North Africa for years and the Castro regime continues its executions. There are countless other examples of our inability to deal with our fellows to our mutual satisfaction. I can only conclude that these failures are indicative of a lack of recognition of the urgency of the situation.

That eminent historian Mr. Arnold Toynbee has stated that he believes we must either establish a workable world government or experience mass suicide. This is certainly a dramatic statement of alternatives. I think that in the long view I tend to agree with Mr. Toynbee. Certainly, I cannot see how a rational mind can consider these two choices as equally attractive.

I am not advancing the proposition of world government as the only, or most feasible, solution. I know there are many reasons why people are afraid even to consider it seriously. It is entirely certain that it will not come simply, or easily. But I do know something about the alternative choice Mr. Toynbee cites. I learned a bit about the meaning of war a few years back. So did many of you. But already the horrors of that experience are fading from our minds.

In the course of my profession I have had to keep relatively well informed on the probable course a war would take today, and I assure you it's difficult for the human intellect to conceive of what could ensue. Now, a day's casualty figures in the millions are discussed without contradiction.

Today, we maintain quite probably the world's greatest military establishment. Its purpose is to maintain the peace. Obviously, it hasn't succeeded entirely, but it has played a significant part in preventing a wholesale nuclear exchange. This military posture of ours is essential to support a policy of our government and it goes by the title of deterrence, or massive retaliation. Another way to describe the policy is prevention by fear. Prevention, even if by fear, is certainly desirable to no prevention, but it's a sad reflection on the policy-makers of the world that in this twentieth century the law of the jungle still prevails.

I, for one, am not happy with this solution. I am not particularly proud of the human race in this regard. A more satisfactory solution to the resolution of differences must be within the grasp of man.

I believe that this challenge to man's ingenuity can be resolved if it is given the dedicated concentration it deserves. The prize at stake is the future course of civilization, and perhaps civilization itself. I solicit your help in finding the answer.

I have no grandiose blueprint to offer you. I know the way is obscure. But let's make the effort to keep man the master of his creations.

There are momentous decisions to be made. Despite the textbooks, let me assure you that there is no easy road to decision making. To determine the right from the wrong, or the best from the worst, can be a most difficult thing. The issues are rarely in black and white, but in most confusing shades of gray. Nevertheless, you have been prepared in school for the task as well as can be done, short of actual real life experience. I beg you, don't flinch from the responsibility. I suspect that you doubt the importance of the role you may perform. I know each of you won't be a President or governor, nor have you such aspirations. But this one thing I ask you to remember: People are going to be influenced by your opinions, by your judgments, by your attitudes and by your conduct. The degree of influence will vary. Don't forget that even in the smallest amount, your contribution shapes the course of civilization by that much.

This requires men and women of courage. You are expected to have courage, for this is your birthright. And by courage, I mean intellectual as well as physical. You must be intellectually honest, and emotionally mature, to put away those biases and prejudices which mark the man who is afraid to look the truth in the eye.

You must be proud of your heritage as citizens of the most influential nation on earth—a nation founded on one of the most ennobling and profound documents of modern man, the United States Constitution—but you must also be ever humble in your recognition of the responsibilities that evolve from that inheritance.

ROBERT W. BURNS is a Brigadier General in the United States Air Force. He was a bomber group commander during World War II and flew twenty-four combat missions. He is currently Assistant Deputy Chief of Staff for Operations, Headquarters, Air Defense Command.

TO TOMORROW'S DOCTORS

Abraham Ribicoff

I ask you men and women who take the Hippocratic oath to consider with me a simple fact: The practice of medicine is a public trust.

Each of you, in your two decades of training thus far, has been heavily endowed by the people of your community, your state and your country. The teachers of many of you have been public employees. In private colleges generous benefactors paid the differences between tuition and costs, for tuition seldom covers total costs.

Nor will the public interest in you end when your education is completed. Soon you will pass an examination and be granted a license to practice by the people. Public laws will govern your practice. The hospital in which you work will be licensed by the public and may well have been built or equipped with public funds.

TO TOMORROW'S DOCTORS

There has been much comment about President Kennedy's inaugural injunction: "Ask not what your country can do for you—ask what you can do for your country."

"Who, me?" people ask. "What can *I* do? And how? After all, I'm a busy man or woman. It's all I can do to work at my job, raise my family, make a living."

The President answered that he spoke not only of deeds of sacrifice but of the spirit of sacrifice. For the truth is that the corollary of freedom is responsible citizenship—that the United States can be strong only if our free society is strong; and our free society can be strong only if those who enjoy its freedom are willing to act for the common good as well as their own personal ends.

The country is the people—the people who have helped you graduates of today to cure in sickness, restore in disability, protect in health. Your success in fulfilling their great expectations will determine your value as a human being. It will also measure your worth as physicians.

Medicine, since its earliest beginnings, has carried high the banner of public service. Hippocrates wrote, in his *Precepts,* "Where there is love of man, there is also love of the art." There can be no purer statement of professional dedication to humanity.

It is interesting that Hippocrates always refers to medicine as "the art" or "my art." The word appears five times in the oath itself. Now we class medicine more as a science than an art.

Art or science, is there not still room in medicine for a full measure of humanitarianism? For you, as medical graduates, the degree to which medicine and humanity are linked is personal and immediate. How vigorously will you strive to put your carefully built scientific capability to the service of those who need it? How swiftly and equitably will you deliver these services to the society of the nineteen-sixties, nineteen-seventies, and nineteen-eighties? In short, how faithfully will you discharge your public trust?

These are the root questions. The rest is technique and technology—indispensable but derivative. And these are the questions which the citizens of this land are asking you today. For as we seek to build—as we acknowledge that we must seek new ways and find new means—all segments of American society are responding. Each is examining its role and its potential; foremost among these is the profession of medicine.

"America is West," said the poet, "and the wind blowing."

Yes, America is West. She is leader of the Western world, defender of a dream in which we all believe, spokesman for liberty and equality. But how does the wind blow for America? How does it blow for you men and women as you emerge from the swift currents of your medical curriculum and pause for a moment before your plunge into the more advanced stages of professional training? How does it blow for us as we look at the facts of contemporary life that will shape your professional careers?

In a few years, you will come into your own as full-fledged practicing physicians. The new world that is yours to serve will be very different from the world as it was when you began your long preparation twenty years ago. There will be more people, for one thing—a fact for which medicine can take much credit. Medicine, being a cause, must also live with the effect: greatly increased numbers of people to be served. And that population will be very different. Its age will have changed. Two age groups—the very young and the very old —are growing more rapidly than the rest of the population. These are precisely the age groups which consume the largest share of medical attention.

More than this: the very texture of our society will be different. Our cities are growing. By 1970, almost three-quarters of us will be living in sprawling complexes of city and suburb. The supercity strains the political and administrative machinery designed for bygone days of the rural majority. It poses complicated problems in terms of distribution of hospitals, patterns of public health service, and private practice of physicians.

More still: our very design of living will be changed. Three generations do not fit as gracefully into a split level or rambler as they did into the farmhouse or townhouse of yesterday. The family's economy will be different, its members better educated and more aware, among other things, of the wonders medicine offers. Their expectations will be higher, including adequate health care on the list of basic rights. They read the popular magazines—they know about research. They will no longer feel that their health is secure or lives saved because of your personal efforts alone.

Within the medical profession itself there will have been changes no less profound than those in the world around us. Already the surgeon's knife enters where it never could before. Entire organs are removed, segments of blood vessels replaced. Drugs conquer once-deadly bacterial enemies and relax the grip of hypertension and even mental disorders. Hormones ease the pain of arthritis and other chronic ailments. Vaccines shield the body against certain viruses. Less spectacular but no less important, simple procedures have been devised to detect hidden diseases before outward signs appear, while they can still be treated and still be cured.

And the result? You have more to offer than ever physicians did before. You will have still more to offer in the future. People want your services and will want them further. But they do not always get what they need when they need it.

ABRAHAM RIBICOFF

Let us face the fact that often—most frequently among our older people—they do not get it because they cannot pay for it. They cannot pay for the medical services they need. Too proud to impose on their children or on others, too ashamed to seek public alms, they postpone the day of reckoning until the point of no return.

Often too, people do not receive your services for subtler, more complicated reasons. Chiefly, these are the result of slowdowns or bottlenecks in the organization and delivery of medical services. Hopefully and gladly we invest millions in medical research. But a research discovery in the laboratory, until it is applied, saves mice, not men. Breakthroughs in research should not be followed by breakdowns in delivery. They should be followed, as swiftly as safety allows, with cures.

No matter how we look at it, the evidence tells us plainly that we should be doing better. The United States, for example, has slipped to tenth place among the nations of the world in prevention of infant mortality. In this seventh year of the dramatically effective Salk vaccine, nearly eighty million people under forty still have not completed the recommended course of injections. Every year nearly thirteen thousand women die of cervical cancer, a disease which can almost infallibly be detected by a simple test in its curable stages. Twenty thousand American lives are taken each year by rheumatic fever and rheumatic heart disease—diseases caused by a chain reaction which, I understand, can be broken at the beginning and in the middle.

The list could be multiplied indefinitely. Many are blind whose sight could have been saved. Many lie helpless whose abilities could be restored. Many sit anguished in mental institutions who might, through treatment, be returned to their families.

We must not only bewail such defects in our health armament; we must fill them. I say "we" deliberately. For as public servants with different skills—as physicians and public administrators—we must apply our separate skills and hearts as quickly and effectively as possible. Such is our duty in a free society. This is our challenge.

We must examine our respective professions with fearless minds. Searching, we must test so-called "eternal truths" against the unmistakable facts of here and now. We must think critically, experiment courageously and change constructively. We must ask ourselves many, many questions. Some of these have to do with the dominant trend in modern medicine—specialization.

Thirty years ago, only one physician in six considered himself a specialist. Today almost half the physicians in private practice limit themselves completely to specialized practice, and many of the rest are part-time specialists. The "family doctor" is a vanishing breed.

Is this necessary or desirable? Obviously, many of the triumphs of modern medicine depend absolutely upon extreme specialization. But how far can we, or should we, go down the road toward fractionization of the patient—toward making him a heart, a head, a tooth, a set of bones? Can we somehow preserve the values of the old ways—of the personal family doctor—while incorporating the values of the new specialization?

In his delightful essay entitled, "When the Doctor is a Pill," Jacques Barzun points out that "to be alive and breathing is not quite enough. . . . We came alone into this world and expect to leave it the same way. When we are ill, we feel similarly alone in our misery; being sick is a highly individual affair, which makes us long for personal attention, not just 'personalized' on the surface; and this is what our system overlooks, what too many of our doctors fail to understand."

And writing of what he calls "the lost art of medicine," Barzun asks, "The patient survives, but why should he spend his worst moments in an atmosphere wholly mechanical and metallic? If he goes to the hospital, he finds it has become a factory run by engineers. The word 'care' has lost its humane meaning and acquired a statistical one which is not at all pleasant . . . he is processed like a side of beef at the Armour plant."

I have a friend who went to the hospital this February for an exploratory operation. She was frightened—she thought she might have cancer. But she was fairly sophisticated in medical matters and understood exactly what needed to be done. First of all, though she wanted a single room and was willing to pay for it, the hospital was—as usual—overcrowded, and she had to share a room with a very sick lady who moaned so long and loud that my friend couldn't rest. She protested and was transferred to another room. That evening seven—count them—seven different people, from surgeon to anesthetist, came to examine her, ask her questions and get her to sign papers. All she wanted, she told me, was a good old-fashioned family doctor to be patient and tell her she was going to be O.K.

Well, she *was* O.K., and you've all heard stories like this. What do we do about them? How do we preserve the art of medical practice while developing the science of practice with consequent specialization? How do we support the skill of the doctor by more effective use of less skilled personnel?

Another set of questions about that most hallowed of all medical phrases, "the doctor-patient relationship": What *is* the physician-patient relationship now? What should it be?

Plainly, it isn't what it used to be. As the trend toward

specialization moves on, the patient has—as we have said—become the patient of a platoon of physicians. Moreover, in our mobile urban and suburban world, each physician has a constantly changing set of patients.

"The physician's conventional image, drawn from the past, has become an anomaly in the twentieth century," the president of the Arizona Medical Association said last year. "In Victorian America, the doctor was an undisguised individual in an age that respected individuals. Now, in many ways, he no longer shares the common experience of his patients. His very learning has become complex and esoteric . . . [the doctors] are perhaps more and more alienated from the common run of people by our altered relation to them. Instead of becoming a professional elite, drawn from and cutting across every social stratum, at the service alike of banker and beggar, we have drifted into an upper-class status identification that prevents us from recognizing the wishes and needs of the great mass of our patients."

Thirty years ago almost half of all physicians' visits were in patients' homes. Today, nine out of ten are in the doctors' offices. This has obvious benefits in terms of time saved and convenient facilities. But how has it affected the physician-patient relationship? Is it important that the patient be seen on his home ground, against his unique social and economic background? Why, in the Worthing Experiment in England, I hear, even psychiatrists visit patients in their homes, and with worthwhile results. That would be quite a switch for our psychiatrist-physicians.

What is the relationship between the private physician and his community's health services? The big health problem of the future will be care of the chronically ill. These patients go through periods when they need to be in a hospital or in a nursing home or even at home. How can the doctor help

[121]

assure the proper availability and coordination of such services?

What about the process of education through which you men and women are now passing? I am sure that your professional training has been magnificent. But are you equipped to serve as broad-gauged citizens of these United States? Do you have time—do you have the cultivated hunger—to read widely and ponder thoughtfully? For as Howard Mumford Jones has pointed out, "Such science as we have is at the mercy of politics, decline of population, war, and the alternating beat of Yin and Yang. . . . So far as applied science creates new things, art will deal with them as it has dealt with the invention of the boat or the creation of television; it will refer them to the passion and motives of men."

I am definitely not an "antiscientist"—one who deplores the discoveries of science in favor of the beauties of art. Far from it. There is great beauty as well as hope in the giant revolution which has taken place in man's knowledge of himself and of the world. But the literate scientist himself would assure you that deep compassion for man's social or economic problems is at the heart of modern scientific medical practice. An understanding of "the passion and motives of men" is the magic tool of the doctor of tomorrow.

How well are you prepared for your job as a citizen of the world? Health, we all know, is a bond among all people. The cry of a sick child can be heard above the harangues of the conference table. And the light in the eyes of a man made well again or protected against future illness transcends any language barrier.

Will you join us as we develop our programs for exchange of skilled medical people between our nation and others? Will you help us conduct short-term teaching and demonstration projects in foreign lands—information exchanges, regularly scheduled seminars, collaboration on specific disease problems?

I think you can; I think you will. For I have faith in our young people today—in you, our new physicians—and confidence in your belief in the American dream. What's more, I think you will contribute to that dream, will give us your ideas of what's lacking and what needs to be done. I know from my years as a governor that new ideas do not need to come from Washington. We in the Federal Government want your ideas. We do not want to tell you what to think.

"What do you want, what do you want?" his own soul asked Ivan Ilych when he lay on his deathbed, helpless and alone.

And Tolstoy tells us that he answered promptly, "To live, and not to suffer."

To live, and not to suffer. This is our hope. This is the task for which you are equipped and trained. Give it your best. Think of it broadly—hopefully—imaginatively. Thus will you help your nation to prevail. And thus will you live as a whole man.

ABRAHAM RIBICOFF, U.S. Secretary of Health, Education and Welfare under President Kennedy, resigned to become a U.S. Senator from Connecticut, the state which he has twice served as governor. He has also been a lawyer, judge and U.S. Representative.

THE UNITED STATES
IN THE SPACE AGE

Glenn T. Seaborg

THE world is changing faster than ever before in the history of civilization. In science, new knowledge is accumulating at a very rapid rate. The time span between scientific discovery and application grows ever shorter.

In the political world, new nations are struggling to bring to their peoples in a few short years the social, economic, political and cultural development that has taken older states scores of years and even centuries to achieve. In many of the arts, new forms of expression are pressing for recognition.

Youth enters a world in which the rapid advances of science and technology have provided man with an opportunity for a richer life than he has ever known before or for more complete destruction than has been heretofore possible.

[124]

There is an urgent need to help the millions of many lands who seek a better way of life. As believers in democracy and in the dignity of the individual, we must help these peoples help themselves. This is a cardinal point in President Kennedy's policy. To meet this challenge will mean a lot of hard work and perhaps some individual sacrifices. This is no time to permit our lives to be dominated by the selfish pursuit of material rewards. This is no time for irresolution or cowardly retreat into some form of escapism.

But in saying this I do not wish to paint only a gloomy picture. The world before you is also one of opportunity and challenge. I hope that many of you will go on with advanced studies. Others are now leaving the classroom and laboratory to embark on chosen fields of work. In either case, this fast tempo of change will have its impact on your lives individually and collectively. It will affect the future of your alma mater.

A special panel of the President's Science Advisory Committee produced a report in 1960 titled, "Scientific Progress, the Universities, and the Federal Government." I had the privilege of heading this panel.

One of the most important panel recommendations advocated increased support for rising centers of science. It was urged that over the next fifteen years the United States should seek to double the number of universities doing excellent work in basic research and graduate education.

The panel report to the President was concerned primarily with improving the resources for scientific research in our country. I think, however, that the spirit of this report suggests a much broader application. There is an urgent need for research in all fields of learning—in the social sciences, in the humanities—and particularly in the areas of study that will improve our educational system.

We require an increased capacity for higher learning and an improvement in our entire educational system. This need was well expressed recently by President Kennedy when he said, "I want our educational system to be the best in the world because the responsibility upon the graduates of our schools is greater than it is upon any other society."

I believe our goal should be to graduate increasing numbers of liberally educated men and women. What do I mean by a "liberally educated" person?

He is one who is aware of the nature of his physical and social environment and of his own nature. He understands the origins of the world's social, religious, governmental and political institutions and the ideas upon which they are based. He is a person who, because of this knowledge, has some basis for making intelligent decisions to adjust to his environment or to change to a better one.

I would like us to think for a few minutes of the place of science in a liberal education. In the kind of society that you will be entering, the widespread lack of knowledge and understanding of science by those pursuing nonscientific careers can be a serious handicap. It is important today that a liberally educated man be as well acquainted with science— its method and spirit, its cultural and aesthetic aspects—as he should be with the great classics.

Therefore, the graduate in the nonscientific disciplines should have a sound training in mathematics. He should be conversant with the basic principles and major developments in the physical and the life sciences. In sum, he should be as literate in science as he is in other fields of knowledge.

But is he? I fear that he is not because we have waited too long in this exciting age of science to increase the quality and scope of science teaching in liberal arts education. We have not faced up to the new needs.

This condition is one that has evolved gradually. The content of a liberal arts education has not kept pace with the rapid change in our present world. There has not been adequate recognition of the increased importance of an understanding of science and technology. Difficulty also lies in pre-college education in science and mathematics.

There has been an unhappy harvest from our lack of sufficient knowledge about science. There are the strange notions of those who hold that science is going too fast; that the clock should be stopped or even turned back. This cannot be done. Once man dared to question the untested natural laws that ruled him, there was and is no turning from the unrelenting pursuit of truth.

Knowledge, of course, whether it be scientific or otherwise, is power. And scientific knowledge, like all power, has been applied both for the good of mankind and to his detriment.

The lack of scientific literacy can have particular application to the problems of the peoples of more primitive, or at least nontechnical, cultures who are trying to fashion viable sovereign states. The West can be instrumental in influencing the kind of societies they will build, but we will be handicapped by a lack of ability to make use of scientific knowledge and methods.

How widespread, for example, is the appreciation of the fact that intelligence among the races is fairly evenly distributed? The fact that a man lives in a hut in the jungle is not a measure of his potential intelligence. Persons acquainted with elementary scientific principles know this.

A better understanding, then, of the capabilities of undeveloped peoples, an understanding which derives from scientific principles that are not difficult to comprehend, might do much to inspire the Western culture to give more intelligent guidance in the peaceful development of national governments in the new countries.

There also should be knowledge and appreciation of the need of basic research and hence a willingness to support it. These are some of the reasons why I place so high a value on the understanding of science by those of you who do not intend to pursue scientific careers.

Perhaps more importantly, *as a citizen,* you have an active role to play in the solution of the scientific and technical problems of our age. This is true whether you become an artist, an industrialist, an administrator, or a housewife and mother.

The civilized man, an individualist, liberally educated, with knowledge of scientific principles, will use his influence and his vote intelligently to prevent our society from taking steps in the direction of an Orwellian 1984. There are a host of national and international problems that press on us for solution. These solutions will tax the resources of the most creative talent of the scientist and the engineer and, at the same time, require political action in which you, as a citizen, should participate.

Some of the problems that I might mention are: development of more economical means of long-range transmission of electric power; better control or reversal of chemical contamination of our environment; long-range weather predictions including, possibly, eventual partial control of weather; de-salting of sea water to meet our growing shortage of freshwater supplies; exploitation of ocean resources; application of biophysics and biochemistry to the whole range of living matter, and means of replacing our dwindling natural resources.

There is a dramatic illustration at hand. We are launched on an exciting period of scientific activity that has captured the imagination of the world—the exploration of space.

THE UNITED STATES IN THE SPACE AGE

Our space program is broadly based, and is yielding much new knowledge of the earth's environment. President Kennedy has announced, as a national objective, the goal of landing a man on the moon within this decade. We have plans for further increasing our effort so as to explore other planets of the solar system.

Obviously, major political decisions will be required at various stages of our space effort. It is the same type of political action that is necessary to aid in the solution of the technological problems I enumerated earlier. From time to time, national and even state legislation will be necessary; cooperation of other governments and international organizations may be essential; and adequate support of the necessary research and development will require the appropriation of hundreds of millions or even billions of dollars—most of it in the form of taxes.

As citizens in this new Space Age, your country will need your intelligent participation in the making of these political decisions. It is for this reason that we must move swiftly to erase scientific illiteracy. Such change will be a dominating characteristic of the world you are entering. There will be change in the physical and cultural environment in which science will play a major role. Therefore, citizens, your understanding of science will help direct that change so that it will benefit our country and our society.

But there are some things that must not change. Paramount among these are the love of truth and learning and a humane regard for your fellow man. These values will endure as long as men and women like you cherish them and protect them.

GLENN T. SEABORG, a distinguished scientist, Nobel Prize Winner (chemistry) and educator, is Chairman of the United States Atomic Energy Commission.

[129]

THE CHALLENGE
AND THE BROAD VIEW

Herbert A. Wilson

INHERENT in the dynamic realities of our time lies man's greatest challenge and opportunity. Moreover, they decree the role we must play. Further, the forces of destiny provide a context of urgency, for they are destructive as well as creative. In response to these things, a moral power structure has risen, born of the twentieth century, to re-awaken the spirit of man. Yet its adversaries charge that this is a pseudo-moral power structure, derived solely from man's desire to survive and perpetuate to all posterity the selfish as well as unselfish achievements of his own genius. Fortunately, as in this case, success or failure will not be measured by immeasurable motives and intentions but by the consequences of action in response to dynamic realities.

THE CHALLENGE AND THE BROAD VIEW

Doctor Arthur Compton summed it up in three lines: "Powers beyond human control are forcing us into rapid change. We can, however, control in substantial measure the direction of the change. Here lies our great opportunity and teaching responsibility."

In respect to the dynamic realities of our time, and in commitment to the "Spirit of '76," the challenge to Americans has come from the voice at the summit of our nation. With the advantage of modern communication, it heralded a message across the face of the earth. This message is now history, and most of you were eyewitnesses. It cannot be repeated here, but to broaden the scope of my message to you, these lines seem significant at this time:

The world is very different now. For man holds in his mortal hands the power to abolish all forms of human poverty and all forms of human life. . . . The torch [of the Revolution] has been passed to a new generation of Americans. . . . United there is little we cannot do in a host of new cooperative ventures. Divided, there is little we can do—for we dare not meet a powerful challenge at odds and split asunder. Let both sides unite to heed in all corners of the earth the command of Isaiah—to "undo the heavy burdens . . . let the oppressed go free."

Simply put, a moral end is sought; you know the rest of the story. It is now a question of ". . . can do for you" or in the same words rearranged, "you can do for." The answer to "can do for you" is virtually nothing; the answer to "you can do for" is to be found in the dynamic realities of our times. What are they? The list is almost inexhaustible. Let us hasten to identify and discuss at least five of them.

The first reality is implicit in these lines from Raymond G. Swing: "We realize that the peace we enjoy is the absence of war, rather than the presence of confidence, understanding and generous conduct." There is increasing realization that tensions are an expected part of peace in a free society—tensions produced from protests to those resulting from our anxieties for achievement in various pursuits of life. One of the things which has always intrigued me about baseball is the rhubarb. For here is a shining example of how men encounter each other with everything but a physical blow. Yet, we know there are exceptions in this game—exceptions which occur when a player or manager loses his best self and resorts to fisticuffs. The game, however, goes on. What is important here is that, unlike the baseball players, we cannot afford to lose our best selves. Tensions must not alarm us to action which leads to peril. At the same time we cannot avoid tensions at the price of dereliction of duties and responsibilities. The phrase is often heard, "Let sleeping dogs lie." Witnesses to crime often refuse to testify because they cannot face the tensions of court involvement and possible consequences. Too often we avoid tensions in our souls by finding temporary avenues of escape. Too often we are so afraid we will do wrong that we end up doing nothing. Too often we shut our eyes to ignorance, poverty and disease to escape the shock to our conscience. None of this implies headlong action but simply suggests that tensions are a new point of departure in human understanding; for cold wars are the initial alternative between survival and destruction. Battles must become spiritual and intellectual, for they will characterize peace for generations to come. And while we refer here to national and international conflict, the same basic principle must apply to every sphere of human relations regardless of scope; for the best assurance of a world peace which includes confidence, understanding and generous conduct, is that we all must become practitioners and agents of this concept.

THE CHALLENGE AND THE BROAD VIEW

The second reality finds a point of departure in the widely used words of the Earl of Chesterfield: "Anything that is worth doing at all is worth doing well." These words as stated leave us a choice. But a more realistic statement in keeping with our times would read: "Anything worth doing at all will *have* to be done well." The demands of excellence are on the increase touching now upon every area of significant endeavor or activity; excellence in precision and accuracy, the kind which puts man-carrying capsules into space; excellence in leadership, embracing courage, judgment, integrity and dedication. Excellence cannot be had in these times without cooperation, teamwork and willingness and ability to assume responsibility. And we who would be professional educators and leaders might review the words taken from Ralph McGill's column when he had an occasion to quote President Kennedy: ". . . the immortal Dante tells us that Divine justice weighs the sins of the cold-blooded and the sins of the warm-hearted in a different scale. Better the occasional fault . . . living in the spirit of charity, than the consistent omissions . . . frozen in the ice of . . . [our own] . . . indifference."

We obtain a sense of the third reality in the concern expressed by the United States Advisory Commission on Information which goes like this: "If the ideas of freedom are to prevail, they must be mobilized, organized and communicated to the people of the world." While the traditional concept of the work of the United States Information Agency has been that of disseminating information through various media, increasing emphasis is now being placed on people as media. This emphasis is derived in part from a reality which says: The urgency of our times demands that everybody involve himself on the operational level of effecting survival—and ultimately a world of brothers. This urgency

[133]

creates many opportunities for involvement. Young people like you are needed to engage in people-to-people activities. The idea of freedom can prevail through the kind of job you hold. The idea of freedom can prevail through hobbies and voluntary service. Yet, whatever you do will call for special kinds of competence. In a recent conference with a representative from the United States Information Agency, I observed some of their job requirements. In addition to competence in some modern language as well as a specific technical or professional competence, there were these things:

1. *Experience in working with people of varied economic, educational and social backgrounds.*
2. *Ability to maintain good public relations.*
3. *Experience in organizing group activities and community projects.*

Almost simultaneously with the conference referred to above, recruiters from the Civil Service Commission, General Foods Corporation, Lockheed Aircraft Corporation and others alluded to qualities other than technical know-how: Adaptability to change, capability of growth, initiative, responsibility and—attributes of good human relations—judgment and cooperation. The important thing in all of this is that we involve ourselves in activities for which we are best suited. All of you cannot and should not join the Peace Corps; all of you cannot and should not seek foreign assignments with the government; for there is a challenge in our own back yards. Accept it in making friends, in eliminating ignorance, poverty and disease. Accept it in raising the cultural level and aspirations of people. When we do this at home we do it in Afghanistan, Indo-China and the Congo, for these places are just outside our windows.

All of us are students of psychology; consequently, the fourth reality should come easy. It is found in Gestalt psychology where we are told that "the whole is greater than the sum of its parts." The dynamic reality to observe here is the increasing magnitude of the whole, often referred to as the "bigger picture," which is easily translated into "best national interest," "best world interest." Along with increasing magnitude are more parts and recognition of more parts. All of our efforts in keeping with previously mentioned realities will be in vain if we fail to see the big picture in whatever we do. This is not easy, for sometimes we are blinded by sentiment or confused between conflicting values —a real source of frustration. And too often we can hear only the music we play. The story is that a tuba player in a band can hear only the tuba. Proof of this came when a tuba player was late for the curtain for the first time in thirty years of performances. Being late, he decided to take a seat in the audience to hear the concert. The last rendition seemed to have moved him very much—"The Battle Hymn of the Republic" it was. As soon as it was completed, he rushed up to the band stand and shouted, "Maestro, the last number was out of this world—simply beautiful. For thirty years I heard nothing but *Uum bau—uum bau*. For the first time I heard (first few notes). You ought to go out there and hear it sometime."

Concern for the big picture is in our own interest. We must see the whole along with its parts. Through the years Negroes were in the picture but were not counted as parts. The forest and the trees must be seen. We can make significant progress only in relationship to our grasp of the big picture.

The Reverend Robert Cannon, former president of Fordham University, provides us with our fifth and final reality as he addresses himself to youth and the great role they play in molding and becoming the world community:

. . . There is always a buoyant surge of life coming up from below, strong, confident, happy—and ignorant. But part of youth's ignorance is a blessing in disguise; for the difficulties and complexities which we elder ones have watched accumulating over the years present, for them, a normal problem. This they proceed to attack with forces we no longer possess and, as a result, somehow the world keeps turning.

And to help them, there is always in the background "a divinity that shapes our ends," an all-wise, all-holy and all powerful God, Who has a very mysterious and wonderful way of bringing good out of evil.

There is a tendency in each generation to discredit youth. Yet, we know that history will tell us that youth have fulfilled their mission. Moreover, there is some evidence that the world can survive only through youth. It is something of a natural law that youth be protected. If a ship is sinking we try to save the children. Men struggle for their children. Youth are more adaptable to change—less like dinosaurs than more mature adults. History teaches us there is great hope in youth—youthful individuals, youthful ideas, youthful nations. The contributions of youth to our civilization are too numerous to mention, and current possibilities of youth are on the increase. There are young nations: Israel is young; independent nations in Africa are young; America is really young; the American Negro is young. Goethe said, "The destiny of any nation, at any given time, depends on the opinions of its young men under five and twenty." Let us begin today to harness our youth to the service of humanity.

These are significant, dynamic realities of our times. Implicit in them are the forces which the leaders of our great nation have seen. These we must see clearly. Increasing clusters of moral strength throughout America accept their challenge as a tremendous opportunity.

Perhaps I can best conclude my message to you by raising several questions pertinent to each reality. They go like this:

1. Can you accept tensions as a part of peace in a free society and at the same time show wisdom, courage and vigilance in dealing with these tensions and their causes?

2. Are you prepared psychologically to seek excellence in all you do—excellence in your life's work and excellence in your personal lives?

3. Do you sense the urgency of our times to the extent that you will involve yourself in some way to achieve the "good life" and spread it across the face of this planet? Or, will you be too busily occupied with the daily requirements of living? Or, will your aspiration level be limited to a car, a home and choice food and clothing?

4. Do you possess the insights which enable one to see the big picture, or are you hampered by limited focus on the trivial and inconsequential?

5. And finally, you have the chronological age, but are you young in spirit, young in ideas, young in aspirations? Are you young in energy?

These questions are certainly not easy to answer, and only you know the answers. But if you can answer them, and if you accept the opportunities they suggest, then we might come closer to answering the questions Carl Sandburg raised in these lines:

HERBERT A. WILSON

In the darkness with a great bundle of grief the
people march.
In the night, and overhead a shovel of stars for keeps,
the people march.
Where to? What next?

HERBERT A. WILSON is Director of Institutional Development at Tuskegee Institute. A World War II
veteran, he has been a public school teacher, school
principal and public relations director. Dr. Wilson received his Ph.D. from Columbia University and did
advanced work at Boston University.

THE UNITED STATES
AND THE COMMUNIST THREAT

Vera M. Dean

As we read today's headlines about Cuba and Laos, about Berlin and Algeria, we may think that we are living in a peculiarly dangerous period of history, and feel a sense of pessimism about the future. It may or may not be a comfort for us to realize that in the nineteen thirties when your parents were probably graduating from college, we were beset by crises of comparable magnitude, and faced comparable anxieties, as forces which precipitated World War II were gathering momentum.

Then we were approaching a confrontation with the Nazis and the Japanese militarists, while remaining fearful of Communism. Now, after trying to contain Communism for over a decade by military alliances, we face new crises as a new period opens in world affairs.

VERA M. DEAN

It is now increasingly clear that the world-wide, rapidly fluctuating struggle between Communism and democracy will require far more than the accumulation of weapons which both sides (except perhaps for Peking) would be reluctant to use save as a desperate last resort. In spite of their command of nuclear weapons, the Communists, while believing firmly in their ultimate victory, have not succeeded in establishing their influence in those areas of the world where workable alternatives exist, as in Western Europe and the United States, or where hope of improvement has been kept alive by non-Communist governments, as in India and some other countries of Asia, as well as in Africa and the Middle East. In spite of various reverses and setbacks, from Cuba to Laos, the democratic nations are far from having lost the struggle to Communism, and their cause has been greatly strengthened by the liquidation since World War II of Western colonial empires, long urged by the United States. The question now is how the struggle to give all nations an opportunity to decide their future freely can be most effectively waged under new conditions.

Today this country recognizes that it is not enough to use the threat of missiles—either by the Russians in Cuba or by us in Southeast Asia. The United States also wonders whether our system of alliances in the Middle East and Southeast Asia represents a solid barrier to revolutionary changes. We are ready to accept the neutralization of areas now being disputed by Communism and democracy, such as Laos—but only if neutralization can be achieved under trustworthy safeguards. We are willing to accept a ban on nuclear tests if it can be effectively policed, and to discuss far-reaching disarmament, if it can be adequately controlled. By showing our readiness to accept restrictions on our own military power we have allayed the fears of those uncommitted nations which thought the United States might risk war with the U.S.S.R. If negotiations for neutralization, a nuclear test ban and disarmament should end in failure, we shall at least have the satisfaction of knowing that we have gained great credit throughout the world for a sincere attempt to find alternatives to war.

What is even more important, we recognize that our basic need today is to identify ourselves with the fears and aspirations of the peoples of non-Western areas and of Latin America, regions where the struggle between Communism and democracy is most intensively waged. This does not mean, as we learned through harsh experience under the Point Four and other aid programs to underdeveloped countries, that we must merely give more and still more technical, economic and financial aid. It means that reforms must be carried out within the countries we help which would put our funds and skills to work for the benefit not of a few landowners or political leaders, but of the people as a whole—and this without resort to the ruthless methods used by the Communists to develop their economies. We now see that political dictatorship, poverty, disease and illiteracy are the best allies of Communism.

In short, the United States must find some way of supporting those elements in underdeveloped countries which want to carry out such reforms of the existing order as may prove to be necessary for their development—even if these should encroach on our public or private interests. This is indeed a task to test our minds and hearts. For, to achieve our purposes, we may find it necessary to intervene in the affairs of other nations—if only by withholding aid from those which prove unable or unwilling to make internal reforms. And this may not prove easy in a period when newly independent nations are understandably jealous of their independence.

Thus we are entering a new phase on the long road we have traveled since 1928 from noncommitment to our constantly greater and still greater involvement in the affairs of the rest of the world. We have gained greatly in experience, in maturity of judgment, in a sense of realism about what is and what is not practicable in relations with both our friends and our opponents. The United States no longer regards power as immoral. Instead, it strives to find ways of using the power it commands as effectively as possible to protect not only its own interests, but also those of other peoples— and this may involve the use of force. As a leading nation in the U.N. and other international organizations, as spokesman for the coalition opposed to Communism, it faces the challenge of transforming the promises inherent in our own democratic experience into a workable blueprint for the development of societies which are decades or centuries behind us in technological, social and political development.

The United States no longer has the illusion, which was often evident in the early postwar years, that it has the capacity to determine the future of the rest of the world. Nor, in spite of Mr. Khrushchev's boasts, is the U.S.S.R. today in a position to claim supremacy on the world scene. For, in contrast to 1928, we and the Russians are not living in a world where a small group of great powers can wield vast influence and dispose of the fate of other peoples without consulting their wishes. With the liberation of colonial peoples, dozens of new nations claim a voice in the affairs of the world community through their participation in the United Nations. The United States must now discover how, in concert with more and more of the new nations, we can prevent supine acceptance of the threats or inducements of Communism and, at the same time, maintain and strengthen a world order from which the Communist powers would not be excluded but which they could not dominate.

The new problems we face emphasize the need for increasingly closer participation by the United States in the work of the U.N., where the crucial decisions of our times can be reached not through coercion, but through free debate leading to a free consensus between nations of widely diverse backgrounds and ideologies. There are some who despair about the possibility of success in our confrontation with the Communists in the U.N. Yet in the most controversial and seemingly hopeless issue of recent times—the issue of the Congo—success is being slowly, if painfully, wrested from a situation which once seemed to threaten utter failure. This experience should give us hope for the future—hope tempered by the knowledge that no final victory should ever be expected, that no sooner has one problem been adjusted than another arises. There will be no point in history at which we shall be able to say that all crises have come to an end, and that we can live peacefully ever after.

To succeed in what is bound to be a never-ending endeavor, we must persist in maintaining and practicing our own ideals of democracy. We shall continue to read the same type of headlines in the future as we have for three decades. But in meeting the crises of tomorrow, we must not be tempted to think that the use of nondemocratic methods at home might more easily assure our triumph over Communism abroad. We cannot help but be on the world scene what we are at home. We need, not to imitate the Communists, but to develop purposes and objectives of our own which can make as powerful an appeal as those of Communism.

Surely this is not an impossible task. But the task of acting purposefully as a democracy in world affairs requires the highest sense of responsibility and the keenest attainable vision of the future on the part both of our political leaders and of all of us as citizens. The best gift our leaders can give us is their confidence in the courage and determination of Americans to face realities without fear. The greatest gift we, in turn, can give to our nation is by learning to live constructively and calmly with continuing world crises.

VERA MICHELES DEAN, teacher, author and lecturer, has been research associate, research director and editor of the Foreign Policy Association; has taught at several institutions, among them Harvard University, Smith College and the University of Rochester; and is now editing a series of books on non-Western countries. She is Professor of International Development at the Graduate School of Public Administration at New York University. Among her own books are *The United States and Russia, New Patterns of Democracy in India* and *Builders of Emerging Nations*.

THE UNITED STATES
AND THE CHANGING WORLD

O. Meredith Wilson

OUR economy has clothed the statistically average American to guarantee comfort, comeliness and cleanliness, but winds of strange doctrine chill his soul. Although, in the language of absolutes, one-third of us may still be ill-housed, ill-clothed and ill-fed, in all the comparative records of history no people has ever had it so good. Yet we remain dissatisfied; ill at ease; lacking in confidence; spiritually chilled and hungry.

Never was a people in better position to understand the warning, "Man does not live by bread alone." For we have the grain to feed ourselves and enough remaining in our elevators to ease the discomfort of millions more. We have experienced the "affluent society," and remain unsatisfied. Those of us who have been both rich and poor find that on balance we prefer being rich. Because it is comfortable we prefer our affluence, but we have lived with it long enough to know that the conditions under which life is lived are not life itself; that, rich or poor, life can still be filled with meaning or emptied of all significance.

The most common indictment of our country is that we have no national purpose and, therefore, lack the will to act. I do not discover this failure of will among us. Nor do I find us without purpose. We, the people, do have a clear vision of desired ends. We want an end to hunger; an end to race discrimination; an end to crime and social maladjustment; an end to disease and human suffering; an end to ignorance, prejudice and meanness of spirit; an end to fear. Stated positively, we do have a goal devoutly desired. It is peace in freedom.

Our problem is not absence of purpose, but frustration resulting from the failure of means. We have been able to increase the production of our acres so that our embarrassments are not want, but surplus. It is a moral disaster for a country that wishes well of all men to find its stomach full and its elevators overflowing with grain while thousands elsewhere suffer from malnutrition.

The questions that cry up at us are these: Why is our abundance unavailing? When we are so deeply interested in the welfare of all men, why are we so misunderstood? When peace is our constant dream, why do our most brilliant advances in science seem tilted toward tools of dreadful violence? How can we explain to our children that a generation blessed with wealth and means to power was helplessly caught in the drift of international life?

Our fathers began life in what is now a great and rich land, confronted with a stubborn and grudging nature. The first generations, challenged by grim necessity, were determined to provide warmth, comfort and culture for their women and children. Their adversary was always nature; the threat was always privation and want. The indexes of success were always material things. We became matchless innovators in creating means to our ends, but developed the habit of assuming that for any future national want, additional material goods would satisfy.

When in freedom our fathers first erected a government, their promise was a spiritual one. It was concerned with justice, equality and happiness, not production. The facts of life have demonstrated that such a culture, though imperfectly realized, provided the best environment for human progress. We sought conditions appropriate to the dignity and free nature of man, and all our wealth was added. The wealth has freed us from hunger and given us leisure to reflect. The reflection has disclosed imperfections in our system of freedom. But our material prosperity has clouded the glass in which we see ourselves. What is the American way of life? The tools of production? A high standard of living? Or the guarantee of human rights? Is it a jet airplane and automation, or an article of faith: that the blessings of liberty will be secured to us and our posterity?

I believe in America and do not doubt the answer to the last question. Our problem is a matter of know-how. Our will is to make men free; to respect the dignity of man, dismissing as an irrelevancy his color or creed. But our machinery for resolution of problems is conditioned by one hundred and fifty years of fight against nature. Our habits have become obsessively material. So we say, "We will that all men shall be equal"; but when we switch the mythical lever to create the child of that will, what emerge are more cars, more dress goods, more things. We can shop together for nylons, cabbages and cars, but in schools we must be separated. Where the spirit is to be fed, the machinery stutters and produces imperfectly.

Our problem is to escape the tyranny of the years. Our wealth and ingenuity must be successfully directed toward the promises of the American Revolution. But the redirection of national effort will depend upon our universities. They are the instruments we have created because we have faith in the perfectibility of man. We have made them perform miracles for us as we have searched for material things. Perhaps we have not required that they adequately attend to the things of the spirit. Our age groans under two dreadful moral burdens. The first is the betrayal of an ideal. It is manifested in the schools and restaurants of the country, and condemns us; for our behavior denies our professions of an undivided humanity. Our ideal is at variance with our way of life, whether we resort to the Declaration of Independence or to St. Paul, who said, "God . . . made the world and all things therein . . . and hath made of one blood all nations of men for to dwell on the face of the earth. . . ." (Acts 17:24–26.)

From such a divorce between ideals and behavior a national neurosis should be expected. To recover a wholesome and integrated national personality, education is the proper prescription. In Jefferson's language, "Enlighten the people generally, and tyranny and oppression of body and mind will vanish like evil spirits at the dawn of day."

The second moral burden is the fear of war. It hangs like the sword of Damocles over the chair of state at every banquet. It absorbs the time and attention of our best minds in government and in science. The most spectacular achievements of modern space research have a shadowy underside. The rhetorical justification of their tax burden is that the same rockets can deliver warheads. I am not foolish enough to deny the need for vigilance, but I do question our obsessive preoccupation with fire power. This evening, sight unseen, I will mortgage my plot on the moon—no, I will sell outright my claim to any acreage on any distant planet, for one good hypothesis that might promise a peaceful life on this one.

Why cannot a university which can show the way to split atoms or send tons of steel hurtling around the sun find a way to draw men's hearts together or make human sympathy as universal as the human mind? The purpose of the university is to help men escape from barbarism into civilization. The culture we have tried to create here is not composed of things. Our effort at education is a form of secular redemption. We exist to save life from being mere disaster; to enable you to live a life which is above meaningless tragedy or inward disgrace.

We charge you to make good your own redemption. For such salvation you will require an affirmative philosophy; it will not be enough that you oppose Communism or Fascism. You shall be saved from disaster and inward disgrace only as you learn to stand erect, secure in your own faith in freedom; prepared, in gratitude for the education made possible to you by your families and a free society, to defend this freedom against encroachments from the left or right. If you accept this charge we shall have new hope, for an informed mind is the best defense against all forms of tyranny.

DR. O. MEREDITH WILSON is President of the University of Minnesota. He was formerly President of the University of Oregon.

FALLACIES AND ROADBLOCKS

George D. Stoddard

AT times we move forward by knowing what to avoid. In the past, certain fallacies have interfered with economic and social progress. Today I feel that, at long last, we are beginning to shake loose from the consequences of a fallacy peculiar to higher education.

Let us first examine the other fallacies.

In classical economics, two great fallacies aided the opponents of democracy and retarded improvement in the human condition.

According to the *lump of wealth fallacy*, wealth is like a cheese. It is just so big, and, as you bite into it, it begins to disappear. The more people eating, the less cheese there is for each person; in fact, if you are not careful, your portion will be small enough to discourage a mouse. Inevitably, there is scurrying and trampling. Since there is a limited amount of wealth, any parasitic leisure class deserves praise. This false doctrine was more prevalent in Europe than in the United States, for in the "old country" there were few visible frontiers.

As we know, the first fallacy was shattered by common sense. Wealth is not a cheese. It is not a bowl of cherries any more than life is. Wealth is a dynamic concept, with no fixed dimensions. It is a composite index of goods and services produced and distributed. Every bona fide worker contributes to it. Except as a mathematical limit, we cannot predict how much wealth will be produced or the extent of the demand. The young Henry Ford could not have measured the growth of the automobile industry or its correlation with the wealth of nations. The airplane was considered a dangerous gadget; radio and television, a wild dream. Some of us can remember a time when the annual cost of running the whole United States was less than one billion dollars. To the early American industrialist, a five-hundred-billion-dollar economy would have appeared as fantastic as today's astronauts, but now we are getting ready for that number so treasured in fourth grade arithmetic, the trillion!

In general, the greater the expenditure, the greater the signs of prosperity. One man's expenses are another man's income. Up to now, Americans have maintained the highest standard of living in the world. At the same time we have reached high personal and corporate savings, but debts and borrowings provide a tail to the financial kite. Since feeling is comparative, no matter what they earn, most people feel poor. Deeply illiterate countries, in which a person may live on forty or fifty cents a day, are unable to accumulate wealth. They can neither save nor borrow on behalf of long-range projects because they fail to produce the necessary goods. China today, suddenly alert to the causal relation between

economic strength and human welfare, has been pulled off
the course politically and down a blind road which may have
no turning and no happy ending. It is imitating the busy ant
and the honey bee. India, perhaps just in time, has sensed
the fallacy of the lump of wealth. Instead of worrying about
the habits of a few rich maharajahs, India is steadily rising
above primitive means of production. The aim is to get away
from intolerable conditions of working and living. This calls
for machines, for science and education. Somewhere between
the worship and the exploitation of mother earth, there can
be a new form of partnership involving Nature, which is
man, and Environment, which is man-made.

A second fallacy, the *lump of labor fallacy*, is intertwined
with the idea of a lump of wealth. There is just so much
work to be done. If everybody seeks a job, there will not be
enough jobs to go around. In fact, if rich people work for a
living when they do not have to, they deprive poor relations
or needy citizens of a livelihood. Hence we should put brakes
upon industrial and technological advancement. Anything
that replaces the hoe, the spinning wheel or manual labor
in general is to be looked upon with suspicion. Automation
is something to be fought every step of the way, as often as
not by some other form of automation.

To catch this fallacy, we need only look around us. The
machines, printing presses, earth movers and computers of
today shake the foundations of such economic prejudices.
We now know that the bigger the machinery, the fewer the
men employed in farming, construction, or a given factory
process, the greater the number of persons employed in the
nation as a whole. After all, somebody has to design and
build the digger, the harvester, the railroad, the truck, the
car, the airplane and the airport. Radio, television and rock-
etry have already opened vast new territories of economic

demand. It takes millions of persons to service and maintain such enterprises. In foods, textiles, medicine, communications and the arts we have gone far beyond the simple life. Moreover, it takes a vast structure of education, business, government and military defense to safeguard our complicated way of life. For us there is no turning back to simple ways or simple minds. If the going gets too rough we may, of course, lose our minds, but that is another matter.

In this complex of supply and demand, unemployment is a temporary, local and truly inexcusable condition. It represents a failure of nerve on the part of persons, corporations and government agencies. There is so much to be done! Consider: How many houses, buildings, streets, parks, schools, churches, hospitals, public institutions, railroads, highways and airports are truly in first-class condition? What percentage of children and youth really get the quality of food, education, medical care, vocational training and recreation that living representatives of the most advanced nation on earth deserve? How far ahead—or behind—is the United States with respect to science, technology and the ability to influence crucial world decisions? How many experts are we prepared to send, right now, to the forty or fifty emerging, underdeveloped nations looking to us, not for tons of advice, but for solid help and on-the-job leadership?

Coming to the question of higher education, I find a fallacy that has not been extirpated from the main body of our thinking. Let us call it the *lump of learning fallacy*. The cheese I referred to at the start of these remarks is replaced by a textbook, a program, a curriculum, a degree. This strange theory holds that there is not enough education to go around; what there is should be reserved for the socio-economic elite. Having entered the ivied halls, we are told there is just so much to be learned and the faster we learn it and get out, the better for everybody. That is the fallacy stripped of its common concealments. To cleave to it, you must believe that college should be a short-term experience, especially for the bright student. The duller you are the more college you need. There is said to be a divine impatience in the best minds; if you keep them full term to their books and laboratories they will run out of ideas—or perhaps the professors will run out of energy.

This fallacy is, in part, a by-product of the boredom that afflicts so many bright students as they move up the grades to college or university. Teachers tend to ignore such students, feeling they must concentrate on those who are failing. College planners, determined to rescue students from this unhappy business, turn to the other extreme. They push the student out of the classroom. They contrive the all-purpose examination. If a student can pass it while refusing to show up as a warm body and a glowing mind, that is considered a very good thing. It saves the wear and tear of instructors; it reduces expenses. Between intellectual splurges, the student can go carefree.

On the surface all is well, but there is a hidden defect. This defect, I believe, is a misconception of the nature of time in human affairs.

As a former psychologist, I am convinced the time factor is important in learning. The forest-wild chimpanzees of Köhler were remarkably intelligent in solving problems. The chimpanzees used a stick to reach out between the bars and pull in bananas. They learned how to join two bamboo sticks together in a crude fish pole in order to reach bananas still farther away. In fact, the brightest chimpanzees not only reached out farthest with the longest fish poles but also learned not to waste time eating until they had scooped in all the bananas. They were pioneers in anthropoid capitalism!

FALLACIES AND ROADBLOCKS

What happened when wild chimpanzees from the same African woods were placed in captivity away from trees and sticks? The answer was clear: they became less intelligent! It took longer to solve the banana problem and more chimpanzees got a failing mark. Not having manipulated sticks—loose or as part of a tree—they spent so much time with the "fundamentals" they did not get around to more abstract problems.

Of course, I do not claim undue comparability between chimpanzees and college students—only some overlap. We learn by being placed in learning situations. We learn to do neither by thinking nor by doing, but by thinking about what we are doing. If the work of a student *in absentia* is a better preparation for a college degree than teaching by professors who have full access to books, laboratories, and the give-and-take of recitations, there is something wrong with the college. All experience is life experience, but it is the business of the college to make the brief life experience of a student uniquely rewarding. There is a freedom of the mind, an incitement to learning if you will, that calls for contacts with living persons. Time is nothing but the theoretical framework in which events transpire. Experience implies a good use of time. To choose to go to college is to say that you have more confidence in what it can do to you than you have in casual and perhaps misdirected experiences. The college is designed to help you find a sense of future, of preparation, of purpose.

Certainly conditions of learning strongly influence its effectiveness. Learning is not something poured over a person like a rich sauce. It penetrates his cells; it shows up in what he knows, does and is. A college graduate is not only different from what he was when he entered. He is different from what he could have been without college. Of course, we hope the difference is in a favorable direction. In this sense, we need not measure a student at all, provided we know what he is doing and what we are doing. To the inspired teacher, measurement is a belated and perhaps trivial confirmation of intellectual progress already discerned in a student.

To repeat, what is learned is incorporated into the very structure of the mind. The process is not one of accretion. It is organic and organismic. We accept learning on these terms or we get enmeshed in a repetitive process devoid of meaning in human affairs. Practically, this suggests that a college would do well to resist both the short-cut and the pack-horse theories of knowledge. The lock step, which is a considered risk of the credit system, is an unconsidered risk of the examination system. Einstein took seven years to get his Ph.D. Did he go around complaining that such a bright boy should get out of school early? Apparently not! Credits, grades and courses—all are variables. No two persons really take the same course, for what they take is intertwined with what they bring. The Greek philosopher was right: you cannot step twice into the same river.

In any event, as teachers we seek something that will stretch testing to the limit. We seek nothing less than complete freedom in thought and optimum freedom in action; these are the conditions of responsible learning and achievement. The test of communication is recommunication. The person who is clear in his mind can make his mind clear to others. To the ready and free mind, beliefs need not come suddenly and with certainty. They evolve. This evolutionary process depends upon an access to organized facts; it calls for critical evaluation.

It is no accident that most education worthy of the name takes place in areas of conflict and controversy. In times of war, conflict takes place on a nation-wide or world-wide scale, but even in time of peace (who can remember such a time?) there is always the conflict within the individual. In a world of free men, no one man speaks for virtue and no one man for country. There is no safety in a totalitarian state of mind. The free spirit will always resist. If we are to move forward as a democratic society, no person and no institution can safely be kept from criticism.

Accordingly, the fallacy of the *lump of learning* is no idle error into which we have fallen. It dominates routine teaching. It fragments the liberal arts, substituting information for knowledge, and knowledge *about* for performance, creativeness and wisdom. In the lines of St. Louis' famous son, T. S. Eliot,

> The endless cycle of idea and action,
> Endless invention, endless experiment,
> Brings knowledge of motion, but not of stillness;
> Knowledge of speech, but not of silence;
> Knowledge of words, and ignorance of the Word.
> All our knowledge brings us nearer to our ignorance,
> All our ignorance brings us nearer to death,
> But nearness to death no nearer to God.
> Where is the Life we have lost in living?
> Where is the wisdom we have lost in knowledge?
> Where is the knowledge we have lost in information?
> The cycles of Heaven in twenty centuries
> Bring us farther from God and nearer to the Dust.

Surely there is ever more to know. The world of the intellect, like the universe itself, is expanding. We can be as bogged down in a deluge of words and formulas as a dinosaur in his asphalt swamp. If the human brain is to remain useful, we must choose, and choose wisely. It takes thousands of years to show the tiniest improvement in inherited structure, but it takes only a few months of sadistic conditioning to break the habit of thinking. Shock can ruin the nervous system in minutes. A single radioactive second can kill millions of persons. This fantastic disjunction between the respective time scales for evolution, learning, and total destruction should forever put a damper on war or the thought of war.

Other fallacies that, I wager, have secretly plagued many of you during your college career will continue to lie in wait, like threatening animals in a dark wood. I have given only a few hints on how to identify them and what to do. There is, for example, *the semantic fallacy,* the identification of the word with the thing itself. Thus we call a set of performances *"intelligence"*—and proceed to look for equivalent entities in a string of chromosomes. What, says the biologist, are the structures? the functions? What, says the physicist, are the operations? What, says the psychologist, are the behavior patterns? What, says the philosopher and leader of men, are the values? What are anybody's intentions if he departs from the straight path of truth? Is it perhaps first to befuddle and then to conquer? If your education has given you the insight and the courage to ask and seek the answers to such questions, it has served you well and will continue to guide your life. After all, to recognize a major fallacy, or a single example of one, is to add a cubit to your intellectual stature. Today the stature of our university graduates is of concern not only to themselves and their fond parents. It is a source of hope and pride around the free world.

GEORGE D. STODDARD is Chancellor and Executive Vice-President of New York University. A veteran of World War I, a psychologist and an educator, he is also an author, having written, among many other books, *The Meaning of Intelligence* and *Frontiers in Education.*

AMERICAN WOMEN AND THE
GOAL OF WORLD COMMUNITY

George C. McGhee

OURS is a world of discord and strife, of nations threatened, of hopes and successes—but also of disappointments. We of the generation that brought you into this world have not left you a legacy of which we can be altogether proud.

And yet, Americans still dream of a world in which the principles upon which our own nation was founded would apply to all peoples and all nations. We still seek a world order grounded in the inherent worth and dignity of every man, where relationships between peoples and nations would permit the widest possible freedom of choice and action.

Two generations of Americans, groping for such a rational, harmonious world, have had their hopes frustrated by the aggression of dictators bent on world conquest. The United Nations, planned in the aftermath of war when peace seemed assured, has made progress in many fields and embodies still our highest hopes.

In recent years we have come to understand that we can live with all truly freedom-loving nations and that each can, indeed, be an added source of strength for us all. We, as a nation based on diversity, have learned that we can live with diversity.

But we must do more than merely accept and adjust to the attitudes of others which differ from our own. This is but a step in our path of progress. We must go one step further. If we are to succeed, we must create now a vision of a more stable and enduring world beyond the "cold war," a vision of a "peaceful world community" which would provide a rallying point for all free nations.

The concept of world community is difficult to define. It must, in the final analysis, be based on an attitude of mind —an instinctive community "feeling." It will grow among men to the extent to which men are able to attain among themselves a consensus. This consensus must then be made tangible through the association of like-minded men in the carrying out of common endeavors.

It is, perhaps, in terms of the development of this consensus that the real meaning can be found in the education you have received. Consensus among men must flow from a consensus within man himself—among his divergent and often contradictory motivations and desires. Education has no higher purpose than to achieve that consensus—the inner harmony of the individual which makes him or her serene and confident before the world.

To this must be added a consensus within our own society. Foreign policy is essentially a projection of our society and behavior at home. Only as our society is sound and good can our foreign policy reflect and project that soundness and goodness. A successful African policy will depend on how we deal with race relations in our own American communities. If we lend a friendly hand to the underprivileged at home, we are more likely to be successful in our relations with the underprivileged abroad.

But how should I speak of the contribution women can make in the achievement of the consensus which can lead to the world community? You women, although you are sometimes willing to isolate yourselves during the process of your education, do not, I find, wish to be considered in a different context from men. And yet in certain deep respects I feel you must. Of the many universals which can bind the people of the world together, many can best be spoken by the tongues of women.

It is not just that women are closest to the life process itself, but that in carrying out the functions which nature and custom have assigned to women, you sense most intimately life's perplexing diversities. This is so in part because many of you will pass through several distinct stages in your lives.

For example, many of you will want to begin careers, and some of you will continue in them to highest achievement. Others of you, however, will test your mettle in the market place for a brief period, and then enter that different life of home and family. But once your children are off to school, you may have an opportunity to loosen the web of personal relationships in your family and set forth again on some new activity outside your home. Women may lead many different lives.

You, too, are the ones who come to understand best the long cycles of change and growth which no man or woman can alter. Women have a different clock from that of men. They know there is no way to hurry the time of growth, waiting for children to be born or to mature. You therefore know that it takes time to weave the fabric of a close, enduring relationship, or for the seasons to roll by, or for the garden to develop to its full delight. Women in all countries possess this kind of deep knowledge.

In one of her poems, Emily Dickinson suggests my thought:

> Could you tell me
> How to grow
> Or is it unconveyed
> Like melody or witchcraft?

As you create your own families, and as you participate in wider spheres of community and professional life, you, like women everywhere, will know how it is to grow. Even if you can't say much about it, if you have the gift of melody, your families and associates will be led to understand this, too.

Men have less awareness of these matters. Moreover, they are apt to be too immersed in the stormy aspects of business or the professions, where one man's advantage is often gained at another man's expense. It is man who makes war and politics. It is difficult for man to heal the divergencies he himself creates.

By contrast, women throughout the world ideally typify values that go unchallenged. It is yours to create and protect life itself in all its aspects, and nearly all of you will share this imperative. You are the ones who have the sense to know, in this technological age, which toys are lethal. As Phyllis McGinley put it:

> Deciding on reflection calm
> Mankind is better off with trifles;
> With Band-aid rather than the bomb,
> With safety match than safety rifles.

[162]

AMERICAN WOMEN AND WORLD COMMUNITY

You also have a particular role to play as conservers of the community's culture. As mothers and teachers of young children, you will consciously and unconsciously instill in the next generation the values and the teachings of the past. You have the double responsibility to choose what of the tradition is worth passing on and what had best be left as the folly of today and not imposed on the young men and women of tomorrow.

In doing this, you live in an unusually exciting era to use your gifts. For the community of which we are in truth a part is exploding beyond the comprehension of our fathers —and often of ourselves. How inconceivable that over one million Americans would be living abroad on their country's business or on their own affairs! Who would have thought that on nearly every American campus there would be students from Africa, Asia, Latin America and Europe. With their presence they have brought to us the insight of our common humanity.

Only recently the first multi-national group of women from twelve Latin American countries has come to our country on a program sponsored by our government. These women are social workers, public health and rehabilitation workers, rural teachers and small-community leaders. They represent the new era of opportunity which has been opened to women of all nations, and which has led to their more intimate involvement in world affairs.

The fates of all peoples are today tied together in a way we could not have imagined, even twenty-five years ago. With the European countries from which most of us came, the links have always been closest. These links lie not solely in our common past, which our liberal arts curriculum so richly underlines. We are now part of one living, interacting future.

But we cannot be complacent in our reach toward Europe.

[163]

We cannot call ourselves educated if we know only the European past and ignore the Asian and the African future.

The community we must embrace is not just our familiar neighborhood, encompassed within a neatly drawn circle of congenial replicas of ourselves. In every community, if we have the wit, we can reach out to strangers and help them to feel the warmth of understanding and of friendship. To visitors from far-off lands, you can offer the touch of fellowship. Women share more easily their friendship—their joys and sorrows.

In Washington, for example, there is a group of young women just beginning their families who use their few hours of free time to assist the wives of African diplomats to learn American ways of life—from pablum to baby sitters—and how we think and live. In turn, these women have come to know something about Muslim dietary habits, the large family group, the art and culture of Africa. This is the dialogue of the nineteen sixties. These young women are searching for a wider community than their mothers could ever have imagined.

No more challenging to your imaginations, but more demanding, may be your opportunity to live in these variegated lands, where the centuries are telescoped and change can be at a break-neck speed. To bridge the gap between yourselves and your hosts will require all your hard-won intellectual skills and your gift of sensitivity. The wider community will not come of itself, but must be reached for.

And from a community among peoples will come a community of nations, freely associated in a growing awareness of common destiny. This is not a community that enforces one view. The community we seek is based on freedom, which leads to variety and change. We are dedicated to defending the right of people and nations to be different.

AMERICAN WOMEN AND WORLD COMMUNITY

We see the rising tide of modernization penetrating into hitherto protected backwaters of the world. We respect and assist the efforts of many peoples to find a unique synthesis of their traditional ways with these disruptive forces.

We see a world where new groups and new generations press forward toward the levers of control, seeking to turn the flow of economic and political forces in new directions. We must welcome this wind of change. We must help those who want to make tomorrow throw up the windows and let the fresh draft in; even if some fusty relics of the past may catch cold and have to retire to bed.

Yet evolving a feeling of identity in a world of diversity will not be simple. Most of you come from homes of reasonable comfort. By most peoples' standards you belong to the "haves and have mores." We must bridge the gap between ourselves and the free world's vast majority who are poor and uneducated and are now demanding their birthrights as men created in God's image.

We must multiply opportunities for international interchange. These should not be indiscriminate, hit-or-miss affairs, but tailored to individual needs and interests. We must bring authors, philosophers, businessmen, historians, and men and women in other fields together with their colleagues in other countries for discussion of each other's problems and aspirations.

Men and women in politics, public administrators, journalists and other opinion formers, and diplomats should meet their counterparts in relaxed surroundings for leisurely exploration of interests and ways of knitting together a peaceful world community of diverse peoples.

The world's great religions grope toward a similar transcendent reality by different routes. There should be closer interchange among them, designed to find not their differences, which are so easy to uncover, but the threads of common ideals and purposes.

We are the senior partners in the non-Communist world, whether we wish it or not. But we must be ready to welcome and support initiatives from elsewhere, too. We do not believe with Thucydides' Athenian that the weaker must be kept down by the stronger. On the contrary, we seek that nice balance which acknowledges that with power comes wider responsibility and wider partnership. It is part of this balance that the weaker are not to be exploited by the stronger. In our own experience we know this can be accomplished.

Ours is a conception of an open world society. Our vision must reach out to meet the needs of the free world's peoples, not only their economic needs but also their need for respect, for understanding and for a sense of participation in the world's affairs. We must work constructively toward such a world of true community, so that in the end the brash claims of the mockers who would deny us our freedoms will sound hollow, and their true nature will be clearly revealed. And—who knows?—perhaps, as so often in the past, the outsiders themselves may be attracted into our world community and changed and assimilated. Edwin Markham has a little quotation that might fit:

> He drew a circle that shut me out;
> Heretic, traitor, a thing to flout;
> But love and I had the wit to win,
> We drew a circle that took him in.

Achieving the world community will not be an easy task. Governmental policy alone cannot accomplish it. Our leaders of opinion and of our many private groups must also understand and work toward that goal. Each of you must work toward it. It is not merely a matter of a program or of institutions, but of individual vision and commitment.

Edna St. Vincent Millay suggested the vision when she wrote:

> The world stands out on either side
> No wider than the heart is wide;
> Above the world is stretched the sky—
> No higher than the soul is high.

These are deeper dimensions of our world than those of science. Our challenge—and yours—is to infuse the world's far reaches with the sense of human-kind, one in its vast numbers and variety, feeling the identity of human beings, making of this riven world a community.

GEORGE C. McGHEE is currently a consultant to the National Security Council. He holds a Ph.D. (Oxford), was a Rhodes Scholar and runs his own oil company. He has also been a United States Ambassador (Turkey) and an Assistant Secretary of State.

FOREIGN AID AND EDUCATION

James L. Morrill

LATELY I have spent considerable time in India, in South America and in the British territories of East Africa.

Whatever is meant by "cultural shock" I surely suffered when I saw the thousands of homeless and hopeless refugees and unemployed, sleeping on the sidewalks of Calcutta in the cold gray dawn; and the little, half-naked African children in the Mau-Mau country of Kenya, attending school in ramshackle shacks open to the rain and weather, but still almost desperately eager to study and learn.

Lately, too, I have been involved in a serious study of "The Role of the University in World Affairs," made by a committee with such eminent and experienced members as Mr. Dean Rusk, our Secretary of State, and Senator J. W. Fulbright, Chairman of the U.S. Senate Committee on Foreign Relations.

FOREIGN AID AND EDUCATION

In the very first paragraphs of its published report, our committee has said—and I quote:

The American university is caught in a rush of events that shakes its tradition of scholarship and tests its ability to adapt and grow. The United States is just awakening to the fact that world affairs are not the concern of the diplomat and soldier alone. They involve the businessman, the farmer, the laborer, the economist—indeed, every citizen. . . .
[In] the upsurge of demands for independence and economic advancement among hundreds of millions abroad who have known little of either . . . they see education as indispensable to their quest for growth and dignity, [and] at the center of these new educational demands . . . stands the American university.

If you ask, as understandably you might, what possible connection is there between universities and their graduates and those shivering youngsters in that schoolhouse in the African bush, or the myriad illiterates of Asia and their children, there is a good answer to that question. Old Jonathan Turner of Illinois gave it a hundred years ago when he declared that "the whole history of education . . . shows that we must begin with the higher institutions or we can never succeed with the lower—for the plain reason that neither knowledge nor water can run uphill."

"Let us hope history will repeat itself," President Henry T. Heald of the Ford Foundation said in appointing the committee that I mentioned. "As American education once rose to the challenge of a young and expanding democracy," he said, "so must it rise to the challenge of a world bursting for brotherhood, knowledge and hope."

Today we find ourselves rudely awakened, not to Homer's "rosy-fingered dawn" but to what my friend, Detlev Bronk, has called the "jet-powered dawn." Every day, as some wag

[169]

said, it seems to take less time to fly the ocean, but longer to drive to work and find a place to park.

Last New Year's, when the newspapers and magazines were full of prophecies for the future, I read the prediction of a noted French authority on aviation. Jet passenger-planes, he said, will fly at Mach 3 in the next ten years—three times the speed of sound.

You can leave Paris at 11:00 a.m., having had your breakfast, he said, and because of the time zone difference you will arrive in New York at 8:20 a.m., just in time for breakfast. You can then leave New York for Los Angeles, arriving out there at 7:45 a.m. for another early breakfast!

And so this whole wide—yet smaller—world is literally at our doorstep. Distance has disappeared. We find ourselves perilously confronted and outnumbered by peoples with whom we must deal and problems we must somehow solve (if only in self-defense) with greater insight and understanding and good will.

And this isn't easy, for, as philosopher Alfred North Whitehead once wrote, "the love of humanity as such is (often) mitigated by violent dislike of the next-door neighbor." Does Cuba, or even Canada, come to mind?

Truly, as someone has said, we are all of us passengers on the same planet, and it is a troubled and turbulent passage that we share. The international climate, the weather through which this country must plot its flight, is rough! As Dean Julius Nolte of Minnesota said recently, the skies are cloudy, the humidity is high, the barometer is falling and the wind is rising.

We may as well face it. Our hopes of "mutual security" are a long way from realization. But there is some reassurance, I think, in something that Whitehead also wrote long before our present perplexities. "The middle class pessimism over the future of the world comes from a confusion between civilization and security," he said; and then he added, "In the immediate future there will be less security, less stability. It must be admitted there is a degree of instability which is inconsistent with civilization. But, on the whole, the *great* ages have been unstable ages."

If we are to think of civilization as the Spanish scholar, Ortega y Gasset, defined it—"above all, the will to live in common"—then the endeavor to create that will is the job of our foreign policy and foreign aid. And what better reliance to this end than educational aid and exchange?

Despite good beginnings, the schools and colleges of this country are just awakening to the greatest educational challenge of the twentieth century—the summons to see outside the Western world of our nurture and knowledge; to train our young people, as we older ones never were trained, to meet the problems and prospects of this dangerously divided world; to upgrade, through education, our own capacities and those of peoples everywhere for responsible self-government and freedom, for productive and peaceful partnership.

Can we somehow help others to learn the lessons we have learned? . . . The lesson, as Thomas Jefferson phrased it, that "no nation can be both ignorant and free"? . . . The lesson of the Congo that stares us in the face—the lesson, as Goethe said, that "there is nothing more frightful than ignorance in action"? . . . The lesson, as Whitehead also wrote, that "in the conditions of modern life, the rule is absolute: the race that does not value trained intelligence is doomed"?

I wonder if we fully realize what it means that while two out of three American children now graduate from high school, of the earth's 550,000,000 children only three hundred million have any schools at all to go to. . . . That not as many as fifty-five per cent of the world's people can read or write a simple sentence in their own language. . . . That in Tanganyika—next door to the Belgian Congo, but infinitely better off educationally—four hundred thousand children do start school, but at the end of the eighth grade only forty thousand remain, and of these only four thousand finish high school.

Out there in East Africa there are actually people who still know nothing about the use of the wheel. Their travel is limited to a day's walk, their knowledge of other people to those of the same tribe in a valley village twenty miles away.

How sobering to reflect that the future of our country, of the free world indeed, could be determined, long-range, by these untutored hundreds of millions—that it is already being determined in some measure today by the new nations' votes in the United Nations!

It's a massive job of education—our own re-education as well as the education of others—that offers the best hope. We are late in learning, ourselves. Some history, a small reading knowledge of a European language, a glimpse of geography —these things most of us have had in college.

"Now we must know something about the literature of Asia and other countries," President Peter Sammartino of Farleigh Dickinson University has well reminded us. "In philosophy and religion our knowledge should include something about Islam, Buddhism, Hinduism and even animism. The economic geography of all continents takes on major importance."

If we buy less manganese from Ghana because our steel production is less, then the economics of Ghana becomes, nowadays, our problem, he went on to say. We are finding out that we need to know about—and reckon with, as never before—the economic interdependence of nations.

With President C. W. de Kiewiet of the University of Rochester, I am persuaded that the deepest division in the modern world is not really so much between democracy and Communism as between the underdeveloped and the developed areas.

The great masses of the illiterate are not yet ready to understand or appreciate the doctrine of democracy or of freedom—of *uhuru,* the kind of freedom for which so many of the hysterical hordes of African tribesmen cry—for democracy presupposes a literate populace.

That is Nehru's problem in India today. It is not ideology but economics that makes the Communist message so attractive—the message which promises the masses a share of the wealth and goods of those who have plenty. To be sure, economic aid overseas is a "must," but steel mills and dams and tractors are no adequate answer to the problem of "mutual security" in the world today.

More and more it is realized that foreign aid must carry a larger emphasis upon education; that human resources are the critical component of the natural resources of any country; that investment in education is investment in the indispensable resource of human ability and competence and hope—the key to economic development and political stability.

Per capita national income corresponds directly with the levels of literacy and education the world over. That has been the American experience, accounting largely for our world leadership today. The Russians are imitating it like mad! What you, your families and the taxpayers have invested in your education has been the soundest investment they could possibly make in the future of the state, the nation, the youth of today and the children of tomorrow.

And more and more it is realized, as a British writer said, that "Universities are central power stations for generating and distributing the voltage and current for the forces of progress." What we have been doing we in the universities must do vastly more of, and better!

Foreign area studies, knowledge of the history and culture and economics of regions we have rarely studied, training in languages we never thought we would need to know, undergraduate and specialized graduate and professional training enlarged and inspired to the dimensions of world understanding—with the likelihood that thousands of you and other graduates sometime will serve in far-off places—these are the sudden summonses to American higher education.

The Russians mean business about their kind of education, at home and for export! In one African schoolhouse I saw the picture of the largest, most impressive building in the whole Soviet Union—the thirty-six story, three hundred million dollar University of Moscow. In the far-off fabled island of Zanzibar, we saw at the airport a group of young Arabs and Africans embarking, via Cairo and Prague, for the new "Friendship of Peoples" university which opened recently in Moscow.

In India, happily, the turn is toward us. Ten years ago India sent its many hundreds of students for training abroad to Great Britain first, Germany second, and the United States third. Today our country gets the largest number, with Britain second and Germany third, I was told in New Delhi.

Ours—not the Russians'—is the rallying cry for freedom and justice. Human welfare in this troubled time depends everywhere—as it depended in our country—upon the conjunction of learning and technology with democratic freedom. As our Committee on the University and World Affairs has said, without learning and technical power, men are slaves to raw nature; without freedom, slaves to each other.

Actually our universities and their graduates are not asked to undertake a really new assignment, but only to expand our horizon and to accept the larger opportunities and obligations so plain to see in that wider view.

Nor is it chauvinism, I think, to say that the American university has made its own significant contribution to the older tradition of the university as a place of learning principally for learning's sake itself—to the idea of the university as a special stronghold of freedom among all the institutions of society.

To this we have added the wider open door of educational opportunity, the idea of "knowledge for use," of responsive service to a needful and changing society. It is this *American* identity which is worthy of transplantation to other lands, I deeply believe.

How often to the poet we turn for the gifts of prescience and prophecy! Walt Whitman, sensitive above all to the American destiny, comes to mind:

> Sail, sail thy best, ship of Democracy—
> Of value is thy freight, 'tis not the Present only,
> The Past is also stored in thee;
> Thou holdest not the venture of thyself
> Alone, not of the Western continent alone—
>
> Earth's *résumé* entire floats on thy
> Keel, O Ship—is steadied by thy spars;
> With thee Time voyages in trust;
> The Antecedent nations sink or swim with thee . . .

JAMES L. MORRILL

Steer then with good strong hand and wary eye,
O Helmsman—Thou carriest great companions:
Venerable priestly Asia sails this day with thee,
And royal feudal Europe sails with thee.

JAMES L. MORRILL, currently Consultant to the Ford
Foundation, has also been President of the University
of Minnesota. He is an authority on news media, communications and education, and has been reporter,
editor and correspondent for various newspapers.

OUR RESPONSIBILITY
TO LATIN AMERICA

The Rev. W. Patrick Donnelly, S.J.

To be an American in the next few years you must have an international viewpoint.

The leaders of the new generation are men who understand the importance of Europe and Asia to the security of the United States; men who realize the necessity of cooperation with rising nations of Africa; men who know the necessity, present and immediate, of building bridges in Latin America. It is of this last topic, Latin America, that I wish to speak to you now.

As President John Kennedy campaigned for election, he constantly insisted upon the importance to the United States of the southern continent of the Western Hemisphere. Repeatedly he said, and I quote him, "I attach to Latin America an importance second only to defense." The reasons this administration has placed such pre-eminence on Latin America are clear and manifest. They apply to all America and doubly so to Louisiana. These people are our closest international neighbors and most influential friends. Look out from gulf port windows of Baton Rouge, Lake Charles or New Orleans to the twenty countries of Latin America and you see a population of 180,000,000, growing much faster than our own. You see nations which possess natural resources unmatched anywhere in the world; and yet millions of their people live in the direst poverty only because they need the help and guidance of the United States as a friend and partner working out their very real problems together.

Our own military defense is inextricably tied up with the Monroe Doctrine, however modified, and with the control of hemispheric sea-lanes by friendly powers, particularly in the area of the Panama Canal. More than fifty per cent of the export trade of the United States goes to Latin America, and the economic investment of the United States businessman to the south of us is something over ten billion dollars.

Accordingly, in terms of neighborliness and all that that implies, in terms of our fellow man and his betterment and advancement—as well as in the glare of enlightened self-interest as reflected in our defense posture—our future economic and cultural development and our national history are inextricably tied up with the history of the twenty nations to the south of us. It is not too much to say that the future of the United States and, for that matter, by implication, the future of the world, is bound up with what the United States does in the next few years in Latin America and—of equal importance—*how we do it.*

Communism has already established a bridgehead ninety miles from the American mainland. In one respect, Castro has started a revolution that has been different from any of the countless other revolutions in Latin American countries. As one Latin American diplomat put it, "Castro went outside the family." For the first time, Russia has been invited in as a friend and governmental partner in Latin America. Latin America already is the closest battleground between America and Russia and will become more so in the next few years. Wasn't it Mr. Khrushchev who announced recently that the Monroe Doctrine was dead?

Until now, we have almost neglected Latin America. The countries to the south of us were expressly excluded from the Marshall Plan in 1948. In the postwar world, the United States devised a two-pronged program: the rehabilitation of destroyed nations and the building up of underdeveloped countries. We did a magnificent service in rehabilitating Europe and the destroyed economies of the nations directly affected by the war. No more glorious chapter exists in the annals of world history than the United States record in this regard.

Our country, too, has worked hard on this second part of the plan, namely, the building up of the underdeveloped countries in the Middle East and East. However, up until now we have tragically neglected and excluded from the program our best friends and our closest associates nearer home. In the light of the torch of Mr. Castro's revolution, the United States has almost been forced to the realization of the need for bridging great gaps and making great moves in building up the underdeveloped Latin American nations.

We see now—and fortunately it is not too late—the need for turning our attention to South America, to build bridges to better understanding, better planning and better action.

The first step, the first bridge, is knowledge. Get the facts, know the picture, favorable or unfavorable, as it exists in

Latin America. The second bridge is the working out of a plan or program that will make the United States an understanding and sympathetic partner to Latin America. The third bridge is action—implementing the program with deeds.

There are several barriers or obstacles to bridge-building in Latin America. The first is one of language or communication. While not of crucial importance, this does point out to educators the necessity of emphasizing the teaching of Spanish in our colleges, high schools and even grammar schools. The day is near when Americans should become bilingual, knowing English and Spanish.

Another obstacle to full understanding is the failure to appreciate the different traditions and cultures. Latin America's culture is mainly Spanish and Portuguese. Our own culture derives largely from the Anglo-Saxon.

The third barrier to this gaining of knowledge exists in the very magnitude of Latin America and the complexity of its history. Twenty countries are involved. One of them, Brazil, is as large as continental United States.

These are obstacles, not to the experts, but to people like you and me. When the ordinary people come to a clear knowledge of Latin America and the need for improvement, action will follow on the highest levels. It seems to me a knowledge of the following facts is essential to the ordinary citizen like you and me—all the more so, when we realize they are common denominators and apply quite generally to all of Latin America:

Fact one: Most of Latin America is made up of one-product countries, countries concentrating on one product such as petroleum, or bananas, or sugar, or copper, or tin. It is not good for one product to dominate any country's economy. We can recall our own difficulties when only cotton was king in the South. There is need for diversity.

Fact two: Society in Latin America is made up of the very rich and the very poor. Between the very rich at one end of the social scale and the far greater masses of very poor at the opposite end, there is no great middle class. There is need, therefore, to bridge this gap. There must be a program that will help distribute the ownership and the use of land much more widely and equitably. There is imperative need for schools and for low-cost housing; a crying need for hospitals and sanitation and sewerage and water facilities. Education for the masses, manual training schools and better agricultural methods can no longer be delayed.

Fact three: Common to all Latin American countries is the very rough topography which so mightily influences their economics. Great distances, mountainous terrain and poor communication tend to retard and isolate vast regions, even whole countries. There is need for bridge-building, road-building, and the building up of communications. The United States has no peer in coping with these kinds of difficulties.

Fact four: Another general fact applicable to nearly all of Latin America is the great hiatus between real democracy and sham democracy or dictatorship. There is a growing imperative to make democracy genuine and representative of the mass of the people. Possibly, because of this lack of democracy, the military has assumed undue importance in some countries. Latin America is almost wasting its substance in tremendous and unnecessary military installations. It is estimated that in a large percentage of countries of Latin America twenty per cent of the budget goes to the military.

I believe we can say that in general these four facts outline and pinpoint the main needs clamoring for solution in Latin America. We as ordinary citizens ought to give our support and encouragement to a program looking to their solution.

[181]

THE REV. W. PATRICK DONNELLY, S.J.

To this effort, the new National Administration must dedicate its energies, and we, as helping citizens, must dedicate our own. We need a U.S. Undersecretary of State for Latin American Affairs, elevating the position to a place of responsibility commensurate with its importance. It has even been suggested by one student of Latin America that our President might dramatically call a meeting in Washington of all of the presidents of Latin America as a striking indication of our knowledge of the needs, and our determination to adopt useful plans in working out our problems as *partners* with the Latin American nations and implement them in a practical way in the near future. The time to do this is not next year; it is now.

The United States can bridge these gaps—America must bridge these gaps if we are not all to fall into the chasm that yawns between us. Vast plans are called for to cope with the facts I have called to your attention. Needed are banking facilities, loans and assistance on a scale much broader than the five hundred million allotted recently in the so-called Bogotá Plan.

Student exchange programs can be increased, and in the long run it may be the most effective of all programs. Actually, Russia seems to realize this. Last year Moscow awarded more than a thousand scholarships to Latin American students. We can hardly do less. The student bridge may indeed be the most important and enduring of all our bridge-building in Latin America.

Without issuing a commercial on behalf of any airline or steamship company, let me suggest that, if at all possible, you personally visit Latin America to help as an individual in seeing the need and working out the program.

Columbus discovered America nearly five hundred years

ago. North America—and you—must now discover South America.

THE REVEREND W. PATRICK DONNELLY, S.J., is president of Jesuit High School, El Paso, Texas, and was formerly president of Loyola University, New Orleans, Louisiana. Father Donnelly is an author (*St. Cyprian —an Early Christian Document* and *Padre of Proletariat*) and an experienced leader of youth in education.

THE UNITED STATES
AND THE U.S.S.R.

Adlai E. Stevenson
[Prefatory remarks deleted]

FORTY years ago, when I graduated from college, all the orators and all the listeners agreed that the world was in excellent condition and the prospects for everlasting peace and prosperity were excellent. A great war had been won to save democracy; the League of Nations had been created to make another war impossible; and the dreams of most of us were bathed in a golden glow of perpetual peace and prosperity.

Those dreams didn't last, as you know. Within a decade this nation—indeed, the whole world—was in the depths of depression, to be followed by war and cold war. The burdens are with us yet and will very likely be with us for years to come. They are a part of the price of being a powerful nation—but not all-powerful—in a world of turmoil and change.

THE UNITED STATES AND THE U.S.S.R.

And since you young people must carry those burdens— in taxes, in military service, in countless services which your country will ask of you—I wouldn't blame you for asking yourselves very seriously what it is all for, and what destination your generation may hope to reach through all these exertions.

It would be foolish to try to prophesy the shape of things to come in a world afflicted with war and near war, with erratic markets, fragile economies, instable alliances and aggressive communism. No nation, however powerful, can subdue all the tides of history to its will. But if we study the tides, and if we have some idea of our own aim, we can try at least, as Jacques Maritain once wrote, "to raise new currents in the flood of circumstance."

What, then, is the international aim of the United States? Are we willing to accept a Communist world empire or, for that matter, a world empire under any power? Certainly not. We don't even want an empire of our own. Nor are we content to live indefinitely armed to the teeth in a bipolar world, trying by a balance of mortal threats to preserve a measure of peace and freedom. That isn't good enough.

No, what I believe we are striving toward, however haltingly, is something much more intricate and much more tolerant than empire—but less dangerous and less highly charged than this present state of cold war. Perhaps the best word for it is *community*.

The obstacles to a real community of nations are many. In the diplomatic struggles at the United Nations, the focus right now is in the colonial and ex-colonial regions, especially Africa. The independence movement has swept a billion people on to the stage of history since the second World War, and its force is irresistible. Our own efforts, at the United Nations and elsewhere, are aimed at channeling these

[185]

enormous new energies in directions which will liberate rather than destroy; which will build bridges of cooperation, instead of digging gulfs of mistrust, between continents and regions, between rich and poor, between black and white.

This takes an infinity of patient diplomacy on both sides. It also will take time—decades at best, even if we use the time given to us to the best advantage. But what we hope to produce will be a result noble enough to warrant all the efforts and frustrations: a new international order in which the old empires are replaced not by still another wave of empires, but by a community of the equal and the free and the tolerant.

But beyond this great post-colonial evolution, which is now at the center of the stage, lies another huge challenge: the hostile and still militant power of the Soviet Union. Ultimately the community must deal successfully with that challenge if there is to be real peace in the world.

I have great hope that this problem too, huge as it is, will be solved as the years go by. It will be solved not by our side seeking to conquer or to dominate the Soviet Union— but by the Soviet Union deciding, in its own interest, in countless small steps from day to day and from year to year, to join the rest of us in building a world of open societies.

In these few minutes, therefore, I would like to reflect with you on just what the open society means for world peace. For this is one of the great issues which will condition your lives for many years to come. I am concerned with the longer run. In the long time scale of years and decades there are forces at work which make few headlines because they are so huge and we are so close to them that we can scarcely perceive them—any more than the early mariners could perceive the roundness of the world on whose surface they sailed.

THE UNITED STATES AND THE U.S.S.R.

It is time for us, then, to climb the mast—or even into the outer heavens!—and study the great globe itself. In such a long perspective I should like to think with you about the biggest country on the face of the globe, the Soviet Union.

Many years ago, in the early days of the revolution, I spent some time in the Soviet Union. Four years ago I traveled there again and very extensively. I talked with Mr. Khrushchev and many senior officials in Western Russia, in Central Asia, in Eastern Siberia; and although we disagreed a good deal, nobody lost his temper and I was most hospitably received. It is a wonderful, puzzling, frustrating country. The people are warmhearted and hospitable, and filled with devotion and pride in their country. Having known so much suffering in war, they are deeply anxious for peace. Pleased with the improvements in their material lives since Stalin, they were hungry for more.

Wherever I went I was literally overwhelmed by the people's friendliness and curiosity about the United States. Yet, alas, enmity, mistrust and misunderstanding have been the official policy for decades, and the question is how to get through that enmity to establish a real peace.

We know that the only *short* road, by way of nuclear war, is suicidal and is thus closed to both sides. All the other roads are long and arduous. The diplomacy of safeguarded disarmament is one. Germany is another. Peaceful trade is another. Creative cooperation in the United Nations, in aid to emerging nations, in peaceful use of outer space—these roads all lead toward peace.

But our troubles with the Soviet Union far transcend the traditional realm of diplomacy, and it may well be outside that realm—or in a new kind of diplomacy, at any rate— that the best road to their solution will be found. The road I have in mind is one which our diplomacy has only recently begun to reconnoiter: namely, direct relations between the *people* of the Soviet Union and the *peoples* of the outside world—from whom, even today, they remain almost entirely cut off.

This is the road to an Open World. Possibly it will prove the longest road of all; but if we dare to travel it, as I think we must, we may find that the longest way round is the shortest way home.

No small part of the ills of today's world stem from the closed society of the Soviet Union. This closedness—the exclusion of the outer world, the suppression of dissent, the control of personal movements, the secrecy and suspicion— all this goes far back into Czarist Russian history. In the last few years, happily, it has been receding—but so far only a little.

Today that closed society is not only an anachronism; it is a danger to peace when all the peoples of the world, in their rapidly increasing numbers, are being pushed into ever-closer contact by the triumphs of science—global communications, modern air transportation, television by satellite, and all the rest. At the same time science has also placed in the hands of the strongest nations, for the first time in history, an almost limitless power of destruction.

And it is at this fateful moment that one of those strongest nations, the Soviet Union, whose people have so much to contribute to the community of mankind, keeps itself sealed off behind an iron curtain; requires its ill-informed citizens to live in daily fear of imaginary enemies; and proclaims that those imaginary enemies will continue to threaten its existence—until the whole world has been remade in the Soviet image. And, of course, by its attempts to remake the world it has made real enemies where none had been before.

Such are the tragic works of closed minds. Russia has

no monopoly of them, of course. Every society, I suppose—including ours—has individuals who hunger for conflict, who seem to get a positive joy out of having an enemy to hate and destroy and will doubtless miss the cold war when it finally ends. Indeed it is a rare individual who has in him none whatever of this warrior urge! But a closed society goes one fatal step further. It elevates the closed mind into an official requirement; it ordains struggle and conflict as the highest and permanent duty of the citizen; and it brands all those whom it cannot control as actual or potential foes.

It is quite a job to keep a closed society closed. Consider the radio jamming system which the Soviet Government uses to drown out the Russian-language programs of the B.B.C., the Voice of America, the Vatican radio, and so on. This apparatus includes some twenty-five hundred shortwave transmitters, all of them broadcasting nothing but noise. It costs about $100,000,000 a year to run. Soviet authorities say it is worth it to protect the people from all those "lies," but for that price at least twenty thousand Soviet families could travel through the United States or other non-Communist countries, and find out for themselves whether the broadcasts are lies or not!

In Siberia in 1958 my party carried a shortwave radio and heard the jamming wherever we went. The United Nations General Assembly was then meeting in emergency session on the Lebanese crisis, and among the programs on the Voice of America which could not be heard because of Soviet jamming was the main speech in the Assembly of—the Soviet Foreign Minister!

Then there are other devices. One is *Glavlit,* a state agency whose permission is required for the publication in the Soviet Union of any book, pamphlet, newspaper, magazine, movie or television program—whether imported or domestic.

[189]

Then finally there is the control over the movement of people. It exists both within the Soviet Union and across its borders. When I went to Eastern Siberia and Kazakstan, I was, by courtesy of the Soviet Government, in a huge area, perhaps twenty-five per cent of the Soviet territory, which is normally closed not only to foreigners but even to Soviet travelers.

As for travel abroad, that is quite beyond the hopes of ordinary people in the Soviet Union. I shall always remember an eager group of young Russians who drew me into friendly conversation on a summer evening in Leningrad; and when it was time to say good night I said, almost as second nature, "Well, come and see us in America."

And one of them, standing there in the northern twilight, answered for all the rest with a single, poignant, memorable word: "How?"

By all these devices the Soviet rulers have made their country into a darkened theater, from which daylight and all the events of the outer world are shut out, and all the play of light and music and action on stage and among the audience is controlled by the director.

And just what is the myth which is enacted so dramatically every day in this enormous theater—before 200,000,000 Soviet spectators? It is the mighty struggle of the Soviet people and their Communist allies to build a society throughout the world under the infallible leadership of the Communist party; and the stubborn resistance of a greedy, ruthless enemy called "capitalist imperialism," a shadowy conspiracy which rules the United States, which plots to destroy Communism by war and to enslave the world—but which the common people, led by the Communists, are destined at last to crush.

Facts which support the plot are published in an endless

stream. Facts which contradict it are suppressed. It is taught to school children in their textbooks; to the millions of young men and women in the Young Communist organization; to the soldiers and officers of the huge and powerful Soviet armed forces—and in fact to all the Soviet people by every available means, year in and year out.

Now, fortunately, most of the plain people of the Soviet Union don't seem to believe all they have been told for forty-five years. If they did, Americans would not be welcomed so eagerly, even in the midst of official hate campaigns.

But I fear many Russians do tend to accept the image of an America ruled by warlike imperialists. And, accepting this false premise, they justify under the heading of self-defense all the dangers and sacrifices imposed by an aggressive Soviet foreign policy.

If this is in fact the popular attitude in the Soviet Union —and I have found it so in talks with a good many Soviet citizens—we have little reason to be surprised. The people have a deep patriotism and a yearning for peace which makes them respond with their emotions to these stories. They have no free press, no freedom to travel, no independent way to check up.

Besides, it is hard for a Russian who has spent all his life under Communism even to begin to comprehend America. He has no experience of an open society like ours, built to tolerate conflicting values—containing countless small, independent centers of influence—making decisions by majority rule but jealous of minority rights. Instead, like his rulers, he tends to picture America as a mirror image of his own system—a dictatorship of an economic class (in our case the rich businessmen) bent on world domination.

Mr. Khrushchev himself spoke for that view of America when he wrote in 1959, in an article published here, that

[191]

probably many of his American readers "think that the idea of capitalism will ultimately triumph." He cannot seem to believe that for us Americans capitalism is not a total system of life, or a secular religion with which we seek to evangelize the world. We don't even *have* a "system" in the totalitarian sense, because we believe that the human personality requires a margin of freedom to make its own choices, which no total system can ever provide.

Such a view of life is evidently foreign to Mr. Khrushchev and, to a great extent, to the Russian people too.

Yet I believe they will come to it. History, even Russian history, moves on. The violent, fearful Bolshevik revolution, with all the dark weight of Russian history on its back, obviously felt the need of external foes to frighten the people into action. I believe that the modern Soviet Union will one day feel able to do without that dangerous stimulus. Its people are enjoying more and more security and the good things of life. Its leaders now openly proclaim that no enemy dares attack them. Surely it will do no harm now for the people of the Soviet Union to learn at last that nations can disagree, even about fundamentals, without hoping and working for each other's downfall; that we in the United States do *not* desire their destruction; that we do *not* want to dominate the world; that we *do* want a Russia that is strong and prosperous and at peace with its neighbors, and a wholehearted member of the community of nations.

The Russians have gained much in competence, and in self-confidence, in recent years. Along with this comes a new tendency to look abroad not so much with suspicion and fear as with frank curiosity. I met this curiosity everywhere, and particularly among the students who before very long will be the nation's leaders. There can be no doubt of their eagerness for contact with the outside world.

THE UNITED STATES AND THE U.S.S.R.

Of course there has already been progress in this direction in recent years. Soviet cultural and technical relations with non-Communist countries, including the United States, have grown since Mr. Khrushchev came to power to a point which would have been unthinkable in the last years of Stalin's rule. The United States and the Soviet Union negotiated an exchange agreement in 1958 which was renewed in 1960 and again in 1962. There have been many useful exchanges, especially both in academic and technical fields and in the performing arts. Other Western countries have done the same.

Under these agreements, for instance, Van Cliburn was cheered to the rafters in the cities of Russia, and the Moiseyev and Ukrainian Dancers have been cheered to the rafters in the cities of America. A Soviet exhibition drew big crowds in New York and an American exhibition drew huge crowds in Moscow. American professors have lectured this past year, in Moscow and Leningrad, on American civilization—our literature, our history and our law.

And the full text of an interview with President Kennedy was read in *Izvestia* by millions of Russians.

The mood of the young people in Moscow was shown this spring in an article by Igor Moiseyev, the head of the famous dance troupe. He condemned what he called the "disgusting dynamism of rock-and-roll and the twist"—neither of which, of course, took long to reach Moscow. But then he laughed at the Communist puritans who tried to suppress these new dances; and said, "The slogan of modern youth is, 'I want to know everything.' It aspires to independence of thought and opinion."

What a revolutionary trend such a statement suggests! And the visit of Benny Goodman to Russia didn't slow it down much, either.

There is a thaw, too, in the exchange of scientific information. In the past few years, Russians have presented important papers at world meetings on atomic science and many other subjects. Now, after a diplomatic launching at the United Nations, there are plans for a permanent "world weather watch"—space satellites managed jointly by the United States and the U.S.S.R., circling the globe and giving every country instantaneous knowledge of the world's weather. It would seem that the spirit of openness is going to break some altitude records; and one day I think President Kennedy's plea will be answered: "Together let us explore the stars."

The question is, what should be done now?

The least we can do, with the future of the world in the balance, is to encourage this delicate growth in every way we know.

—We should redouble our exchange programs and make them fully reciprocal.

—We should end forever such an obsolete practice as the closing off of forbidden zones to foreign travel.

—We should hold more exhibitions on each other's territory—not just in Moscow and New York but in cities from Minsk to Vladivostok, and from Portland, Maine to Portland, Oregon. And, if I may insert a personal note, I am still waiting and hoping to see the incomparable puppet theaters of the Soviet Union perform in the United States!

—We should adopt a world-wide rule that anybody, anywhere, has a right to read any document issued by the United Nations and that member governments have a positive duty to facilitate the United Nations information program.

—We should agree that every nation will welcome to the newsstands of its major cities the serious newspapers and magazines of other nations, regardless of politics.

THE UNITED STATES AND THE U.S.S.R.

—We should continue to urge the joint TV appearances of President Kennedy and Chairman Khrushchev, about which Mr. Salinger has been negotiating.

—We should extend the free importation of books, without political censorship and without customs duty, to every nation.

—We should multiply international student exchanges.

—We should see that what school children study about each other's countries is balanced and free from politically inspired hatred and distortion.

—We should let the ordinary citizens of every country, by the thousands and tens of thousands, travel abroad for business or pleasure—and see that there are good hosts to receive them and to help them learn, and to learn from them.

And, I believe, we should do all we can to promote mutually profitable trade in those things which improve and adorn the life of the people.

Examples like these can be multiplied. They apply with special relevance to the Soviet Union and the United States, but ultimately they must apply to all countries. And there is not a country in the world which cannot improve in this field.

I believe such steps as these are steps toward peace— the peace of the free. At the root of them lies a free society's peaceable view of life: a view which is not terrified by things new and strange; which can be a little bit patient about things it doesn't like; which can disagree, even over fundamentals, without coming to blows, because its deepest beliefs are tempered by a certain humility.

We have had enough of systems of thought which cry, "I alone have the key to truth." We have had enough of movements which set out to prove their godlike understanding by dragging fellow creatures through blood and fire. That belongs to the Thirty Years' War, not to our time. The thermonuclear generation would do better to study the humility of Socrates, who said he was the wisest man in Athens because only he, among all Athenians, knew the depth of his own ignorance.

It would be hard to exaggerate how deeply this great issue of the open society can affect all our destinies. As long as doors remain shut between the powerful nations of the world, the arms race with all its mortal dangers is likely to persist; and the community which the United Nations seeks to embody will remain no better than half-realized. What a price to pay for the pride of ideology!

Sometimes it seems to me, working at the United Nations, that the name of that organization is almost right, but that the verb is in the wrong tense. It should be, if we were precise, the *Uniting* Nations. It was founded to maintain a peace which has never been made. It is not something established and achieved, by means of which we casually attend to little quarrels and difficulties as they arise. It is rather a center of aspiration; a continuous process of wrestling with the seemingly irreconcilable; and a constant straining to break out of those temptingly clear but hopelessly narrow logical systems which drive us apart, into a less clear but far wider and deeper logic of tolerance and brotherhood that can save mankind.

How excruciatingly slow that process seems, and how distant that aspiration! But "man's reach must exceed his grasp, else what's a heaven for?" It is not just the dread of war but the yearning for peace, and the intuition of brotherhood, that can exert the necessary force to move humanity, against all the obstacles of outworn institutions, toward a peace based on tolerance. The movement is glacial in its slowness, but glacial also in its power.

And surely, at some point along the way, it will be necessary for each and all of us—Russians, Americans, Europeans and Latin Americans, Asians and Africans—not only to disarm our armies of dreadful weapons, but to disarm our minds of dreadful fears; to open our frontiers, our schools and our homes to the clean winds of fact and of free and friendly dialogues; and to have done with those exclusive fanatical dogmas which can make whole peoples live in terror of imaginary foes.

Not in order to save one people or one empire or one system, but to save Man himself, we must act on the truth which our experience makes inescapable: that the road to peace in this fearful generation—a generation of which you are soon to be the custodians—is the road to an open world.

ADLAI E. STEVENSON, currently United States Ambassador to the United Nations, has twice been a presidential candidate and also has served as Governor of Illinois. Among his published works are *Call to Greatness*, *The New America* and *Friends and Enemies*.

FREEDOM:
HERITAGE AND RESPONSIBILITY

Barry M. Goldwater

I THINK you should realize very early that if we are to win the final decision over the forces that would enslave the world, if we are going to preserve individual freedom and our way of life, a large part of the job will be on your shoulders. I am convinced that your generation has a destiny directly related to this nation's chances of survival and the extension of freedom for mankind throughout the world. I believe you young men and women are freedom's greatest hope in what has come to be perhaps its darkest hour.

This responsibility of which I speak is a charge you should be proud to meet with your greatest energies and your finest thinking. It is indivisible from individual freedom and it is of one piece with the efforts of those quiet, heroic men who carved this great republic out of the wilderness.

[198]

And there is no way to escape it, for the events transpiring at this moment in the world and in the nation are already engulfing you. For the future, they will have a great bearing on everything that concerns you—on your lives, your careers, your hopes and your dreams—just as your own thinking and acting will have a bearing on the generations that succeed you. It is indeed true that youth belongs to the future and the future belongs to youth. But, to insure the future, youth must think and act in the present. And it must look to the lessons of the past and learn what has worked and has failed if its thoughts and actions are to be equal to the challenge. Now you will note that I said *look* to the past and not live in the past or attempt to return to the past. This is a key point in the conflict of ideas which grips us today and a point upon which the future of civilization could conceivably turn.

Our responsibility to the present and to the future is to discover under what conditions man has performed at his efficient best. We must learn what philosophy and what system enabled men to make the greatest possible use of his God-given talents and human energy. We must pay close heed also to the philosophies and systems which have stifled the individual and reduced the industry, incentive and improvisation that breed progress.

This is a process of learning that goes on forever. It does not cease with the completion of your studies, nor will it end with the completion of any future curricula upon which you may embark.

The entire human race, no less than the individual, must learn through experience, for we have no method by which we can project our progress in the future unless we understand the principles and actions which contributed to the past. Without a clear comprehension of the direction from which we have come, we cannot possibly chart the direction in which we should go.

Now in considering the direction of the world over the recorded history of man's existence, we find a very curious phenomenon—a phenomenon which I believe must be thoroughly understood as we move into the crucial stages of the global struggle between the forces of freedom and the forces of slavery. And that phenomenon is confined in space to the land mass of North America and in time to the years the United States has been in existence.

This phenomenon is one of abundance in the midst of want; of accomplishment in an era of stagnation; of hope in a world of despair. It is a story of the proper utilization of human energy, of the spiritual and material fruits of a way of life which has stood the test of time.

Yes, this is the American story which today is the hope of freedom. It contains the only elements of strength which—if they are guarded well—can meet the ultimate test of Communist totalitarianism. It is not a new story but it needs reemphasis in the light of today's crucial events. We need to see it in the proper context, in the proper depth and against the backdrop of how it differed from what men had done before.

Perhaps the late author, Henry Grady Weaver, said it best in his book, *The Mainspring of Human Progress*. I would ask you to consider his words carefully. Let me quote:

For a very long time, this planet that we call Earth has been inhabited by human beings not much different from ourselves. Their desire to live has been just as strong as ours. They have had at least as much physical strength as the average person of today, and among them have been men and women of great intelligence. But down through the ages, most human beings have gone hungry and many of them have always starved.

Hunger has always been normal. Even to this day, famines kill multitudes in China, India and Africa; and in the nineteen thirties, thousands upon thousands starved to death in the richest farmlands in the Soviet Union.

Down through the ages, countless millions, struggling unsuccessfully to keep bare life in wretched bodies, have died young in misery and squalor. THEN SUDDENLY, IN ONE SPOT ON THIS PLANET, PEOPLE EAT SO ABUNDANTLY THAT THE PANGS OF HUNGER ARE FORGOTTEN.

Think of that. Suddenly in one spot of this planet a light appeared to shine bright in the recorded history of man's progress. Why was this? Why was it that after six thousand years of want, famine was banished in America? Why was it that in less than two hundred years one particular group of people was able to do what had never been accomplished before? Why were these people, living on only one speck of the globe with only a small fraction of the world's population, able to outproduce all others combined?

The answer lies in the thinking and acting of this nation's earliest students, the men who drew up a form of government the like of which the world had never seen before. It lies in actions based on careful perusal of the lessons of history, lessons which proved that from time immemorial the concentration of power in the hands of the few had failed miserably to insure freedom or give people the fruits of their labor. It lies in a recognition of the fact that the failures of the past had squandered the most precious of all commodities—human energy—in suppressing the most precious of all rights—human liberty. They were to be avoided.

Therefore, the men who drew the governmental blueprint for America started with the assumption that men are endowed by God with certain rights and privileges and that government's only proper role should be in the protection of those rights. They rejected entirely the theory that man's rights stem from authority, from the state, and proceeded to build in our Constitution something new and different in the way of governmental charters. This novelty was in provisions which specifically stated that certain institutions and human relations were to be left *outside* the authority of government. They actually forbade the government to infringe on or violate these areas.

Strangely enough, not many Americans are aware of the fact that the concept of government confinement and individual freedom had never before been incorporated into a national constitution. And, unfortunately, not enough Americans today realize the wisdom and foresight that went into the framing of the United States Constitution.

Freedom today—as always—is dependent upon government confinement, for freedom can be drained away only through the concentration of authority. This was well understood by the framers of our Constitution. They distrusted government. What they had read of history gave them the sure knowledge that the power of government is always a dangerous weapon regardless of who holds it. And so they took out insurance against concentration and misuse of authority. They laid the groundwork for actual pursuit and practice of individual freedom in the development of a society and a nation. They understood that what could never have been accomplished under a condition of servitude is the almost natural result of a condition of freedom. They knew that human nature is unchanging and that it is so designed that men are only at their best when they are permitted to live like men.

Let me emphasize that these men to whom the world owes so much were not guessing at a form of government that would work in the wilderness. They had experienced various forms of despotism and tyranny and studied others. They knew that the most progress is made when men have been released from bondage, given control over their own actions, and allowed to receive the fruits of their labor. They acted accordingly, and the result is the American miracle and the finest heritage it is possible for men to bequeath.

And with that bequest, an enormous power has come down to you which carries with it the requirement that you protect it zealously and use it wisely.

Our great Republic, with all that it represents of hope and freedom in the world, will be what you make it. Its traditions and principles, its institutions of religious liberty, of educational and economic opportunity, of Constitutional rights, of the integrity of the law, are the most precious possessions of the human race. As our forefathers recognized, these things do *not* come from government. They are bestowed by God and their abiding place is with the people.

And in stressing your responsibility, I would remind you that our way of life, our economics, our republican form of government are not the result of accident or fortuitous circumstance. They came from hard-bitten, experienced men who could face facts and meet responsibilities and were willing to grapple with just such realities as we find ourselves confronted with today. From such men came the sturdy time-tested foundations on which our country was built and which are today the main supports of our freedom and our prosperity. From them came the flower of civilization with its guarantees of liberty, its enormous material resources and its creative genius.

America is much more than a geographical location or a seat in the United Nations. It is a combination and a relationship. It is the destiny of a masterful, pioneering people, enduring all the hardships of settling a new country, deter-

[203]

mined to be free. It is the Declaration of Independence and the United States Constitution, with a system of local self-government. It is development and progress on the farm, in the factory, in the mine. It is the creation of worldwide commerce and the opening of vast lines of travel by sea, land and air.

Our country is truly the result of man's incomprehensible triumph after six thousand years—a triumph of human progress which conferred on its people untold material wealth, military strength and spiritual rewards.

And think of the people who did all this. They were drawn from the world at large. They came from many nations, speaking many languages, holding to various traditions. But they met on this continent with a common goal—freedom. And out of the confusion of tongues, the conflict of traditions, the vast differences of tastes and talents, they evolved a spiritual union grounded in liberty that was to become the first model, later the example and now the hope of the entire world.

And this is what we fight *for* and *with* today in the great crisis of freedom which has split the world into armed ideological camps, threatening our national survival and devolving on you and young people just like you the job of holding high the torch of freedom in a new and perilous era.

You will hear an increasing amount of talk about change— about how we as a government, and we as a people, must change. And I will not argue against change. I think change is necessary and that we should constantly work for changes in our methods and procedures that will improve things, that will better our lives, that will make more secure the blessings of freedom in this country. And, I would suggest to you graduates that you do not improve or change things for the better by discarding basic and proven doctrines.

I would urge you to work for the right kind of change—the

kind that will be positive and helpful in charting the right course for your lives and the nation's life—but don't tamper with the natural laws and the fundamentals that have been tested and proven. There are too many voices in America today suggesting that we change our historic concept of freedom by turning over more and more power to the federal government. There is also a preoccupation with a subject called "national goals," which I find disconcerting because it presupposes that we don't have a national goal sufficient to the realities of today. This, however, is not true. We have a national goal and have had a national goal which is the finest ever devised. It is contained in the words of Thomas Jefferson in our Declaration of Independence when he wrote, "We hold these truths to be self-evident: that all men are created equal; that they are endowed by their Creator with certain inalienable rights; that among these are life, liberty and the pursuit of happiness."

Now I submit that there can be no other national goal than the one contained in the Declaration of Independence, because if we change that, we must change our entire concept of freedom as coming from God and we must alter our entire course of government to conform.

To me this emphasis on seeking after new national goals is a symptom of the disease that ails freedom today. It is a result of man's constant and determined seeking after material things to the exclusion of spiritual values. I suggest that we have become so preoccupied for the last thirty years with the siren call of material goods that cosmetics and TV sets have become more important to many people than freedom of speech.

Those who cry the loudest for basic changes—changes in our economic system, in our Constitution, in our traditions— do not understand the crisis of our time or the anatomy of all crises down through history. They do not want to admit that man with his unchanging nature is the cause of crisis. The problem is man. Conditions are caused by men and they change from day to day, in the world, in the nation, on Main Street and in schools and universities—but the nature of the individual does not change. That nature, with all of its imperfection, is the same today as it was five thousand years ago. Therefore, what man did in history in response to certain conditions, circumstances and philosophies, he will do again today. If it were possible to pass a law which could remove the greed, hatred, envy and other unfavorable characteristics of man's nature, we could easily fit the individual to whatever conditions that arise. We could make man forever noble and gear him to perform always at an honorable peak of efficiency and endeavor. We could make things so perfect that there would be no need for laws or government.

But this is patently impossible, so we must reckon with the nature of man as it is, realizing that some men have an insatiable desire for power and must be restrained. This is what our Constitution is aimed at—the prevention of concentrations of power into the hands of a few who might abuse it. This is the concept of limited government upon which our individual freedom depends. And, it is just as valid and just as workable today as it was two hundred years ago when it was framed by men who had studied and learned from the past—men who had taken the lessons of history and used them profitably as an applied science—men who recognized the eternal reality of rights bestowed at birth on all men.

History contains answers to the present and the future—not only for you as individuals, but for this nation, this world and all mankind. If you study it well and continue to study it right on through life, you will understand the motivating forces of human progress. You will avoid other men's mistakes in carving a brighter future. And you will be worthier sons of freedom than some of us who have gone before you and—through complacency and inattention to the lessons written in the sands of time—have allowed a process of erosion to begin in the structure of our greatness.

BARRY M. GOLDWATER, United States Senator from Arizona, "Mr. Conservative" and a pungent speaker and writer, is also a businessman and an author, *Arizona Portraits, Journey Down the River of Canyons* and *The Conscience of a Conservative* being some of his published works.

OUR NATIONAL GOALS

Douglas MacArthur

I CAN tell you some of the things your teachers hope that your course of instruction has produced in addition to the acquired knowledge and accumulation of facts that it necessarily accomplished.

They hope above all else that it has been a builder of basic character; that it has molded you for your future roles as the custodians of the Republic; that it has taught you to be strong enough to know when you are weak, and brave enough to face yourself when you are afraid; that it has taught you to be proud and unbending in honest failure but humble and gentle in success, not to substitute wishes for actions, not to seek the path of comfort but to face the stress and spur of difficulty and challenge, to learn to stand up in the storm but to feel compassion for those who fall, to have a heart that is clear, a goal that is high, to master yourself before you seek to master others, to learn to laugh yet never forget how to weep, to reach into the future yet never neglect the past, to be serious yet never to take yourself too seriously, to be humble so that you may always remember the simplicity of true greatness, the open mind of true wisdom, the meekness of true strength; that it has given you a temper of the will, a quality of the imagination, a vigor of the emotions, a freshness of the deep springs of life, a temperamental predominance of courage over timidity, of an appetite for adventure over love of ease; that it has created in your heart the sense of wonder, the undaunted challenge of events, the unfailing hope for what next, and the joy and inspiration of life; that it has taught you in this way to be an American.

And what, you might well ask, is this world which you now face? Since you were born it has turned over many, many times. The thrust into outer space of the satellite spheres and missiles marked the beginning of a new epoch in the long story of mankind—the chapter of the space age. In the five or more billions of years the scientists tell us it has taken to form the earth, in the three or more billion years of development of the human race, there has never been a greater, a more staggering or abrupt evolution. We deal now not with things of this world only but with the illimitable distances, and, as yet, unfathomed mysteries of the universe. We have found the "Lost Horizon." We have discovered a new and boundless frontier. We speak now in strange new terms; of harnessing the cosmic energy; of making the winds and the tides work for us; of purifying sea water for our drink; of creating new and unheard of synthetic materials to supplement or even replace our old standard basics; of mining ocean floors for new fields of wealth and food; of disease preventives to increase the span of life to more than a hundred years; of controlling weather for a more equitable adjustment of heat

[209]

and cold, of rain and shine; of space ships to the moon; of the prime target in war no longer the armed forces of an enemy but instead his civil populations; of ultimate conflict between a united human race and the sinister force of some other planetary galaxy; of such dreams and fantasies as to make life now the most exciting of all time.

And how goes this life in this our own beloved country? Two schools of thought exist—the one almost utopian in outlook, the other warning of dangers.

The optimist Allan Drury says, "This land, by the grace of God and the unceasing efforts of its people, is free. The first object of a free people should be the preservation of their liberty. This takes courage as it at times tends toward governmental inefficiency. Some peoples have it, some peoples do not. The Twentieth Century, most violent crucible yet provided for the human race, is rapidly finding out which is which. In that testing, our country, the Great Republic of the West, still stands supreme, battered though she is by the vicious and incessant onslaughts of her enemies and the occasional confusions and wearings of will by her own citizens. Her freedom is not perfect—but it is better than that of most of her contemporaries. Her liberties are not everywhere as thorough and complete as they should be—but compared to the grimly laughable mockeries of liberty that go on elsewhere, they shine like a tenfold beacon in the night. Our errors are those of the goodhearted; our ineptitudes those of a contender who cannot yet quite conceive of the utter evil arrayed against us. We are awkward at times. Shortsighted at times. At times hesitant and uncertain and almost willfully stupid. We are, now and again, an object of ridicule to a carping world and, upon occasion, an object of scorn. But we are free. There is nothing simple or easy in this freedom, which so many peoples shout about and so few really understand. It is only in a few favored lands that it has ever been achieved. Ours is one."

Yet, in deep warning we hear the voice of one of our greatest statesmen, Senator Byrd:

Continuing centralization of government is destroying our freedom and strength. We have already gone too far. With excessive centralization comes excessive central edict, regulation and taxation limiting and drastically curtailing personal freedom. The requirements of free government are simple—honesty and individual initiative, self-reliance and willing work, constructive production and free competition, progressive development with sound financing. Without these there will be neither solid progress nor security. We are being challenged from abroad and undermined at home. We are showing signs of weakness just when we should be strongest. Our strength is being sapped by deficit financing indulged in too long; federal paternalism grown too big; courts grown too mighty; power groups grown too arrogant. These are subverting our system, changing our attitudes and hobbling our will for freedom. For fifteen years the United States has been the world's banker, the world's policeman, the world's Santa Claus. We are showing the strain. We are in a dangerous storm.

And President Kennedy declared in his first address to Congress: "Before my term has ended, we shall have to test anew whether a nation organized and governed such as ours can endure. The outcome is by no means certain."

And all this now becomes your problem. Our two great political parties will divide over you—over what you are— over what you ought to be—over what you can be. The one will preach citizen individuality, the other group collectivism; the one based on the individual, the other on the mass.

If I were permitted but one word of advice to you young

men and women now standing on the threshold of these challenging opportunities and responsibilities, it would be to hold inviolate the immutable principles upon which have rested our hallowed traditions of liberty and freedom. I realize well that it is in the very nature of things that the restless spirit of youth seeks change. But change should not be sought for the sake of change alone. It should be sought only to adapt those time-tested principles to the new requirements of an expanding society. For just as in war strategy is immutable while tactics must change to meet new field conditions, so in peace basic principles which have been proved in the crucible of human experience should remain immutable while the administration for their application changes to meet the requirements of an ever advancing civilization. The problem for ages has been to rescue liberty from the grasp of despotic power. "The spirit of liberty," said one of our greatest past senators, Daniel Webster, "should be bold and fearless, but it should also be cautious, sagacious, discriminating, farsighted. It should be jealous of encroachment, jealous of power, jealous of man. It should demand checks; it should seek for guards; it should insist on securities. It should fortify itself with all possible care against the assaults of ambition and passion. It should not trust the amiable weaknesses of human nature and thereby permit power to overstep its prescribed limits, even though benevolence, good intent and patriotic purpose come along with it. It should look before and after and, building on the experience of ages which are past, should labor diligently for the benefit of ages to come."

And overshadowing all other problems you will face, intruding upon every thought and action, encompassing all that you hold most dear, dictating not only the past but your very future, is the master problem of global war. How, you can well ask, did such an institution as war become so integrated with man's life and civilization? How has it grown to be the most vital factor in our existence?

It started in a modest enough way as a sort of gladiatorial method of settling disputes between conflicting tribes. One of the oldest and most classical examples is the Biblical story of David and Goliath. Each of the two contesting groups selected its champion. They fought, and based upon the outcome, an agreement resulted. Then, as time went on, small professional groups known as armies replaced the individual champions. And these groups fought in some obscure corner of the world and victory or defeat was accepted as the basis of an ensuing peace. And from then on, down through the ages, the constant record is an increase in the character and strength of the forces with the rate of increase always accelerating. From a small percentage of the population it finally engulfed all. It is now the nation in arms. Within the span of my own life I have witnessed much of this evolution. At the turn of the century, when I joined the Army, the target was one enemy casualty at the end of a rifle, a pistol, a bayonet, a sword. Then came the machine gun designed to kill by the dozens. After that the heavy artillery raining death upon the hundreds. Then the aerial bomb to strike by the thousands—followed by the atom explosion to reach the hundreds of thousands. Now electronics and other processes of science have raised the destructive potential to encompass millions. And with restless hands we work feverishly in dark laboratories to find the means to destroy all at one blow.

But this very triumph of scientific annihilation—this very success of invention—has destroyed the possibility of war as a medium for the practical settlement of international differences. The enormous destruction to both sides of closely matched opponents makes it impossible for even the winner to translate it into anything but his own disaster.

The late war, even with its now antiquated armaments, clearly demonstrated that the victor had to bear in large part the very injuries inflicted on his foe. We expended billions of dollars and untold energies to heal the wounds of Germany and Japan.

Global war has become a Frankenstein to destroy both sides. No longer can it be a successful weapon of international adventure. If you lose, you are annihilated. If you win, you stand only to lose. No longer does it possess even the chance of the winner of a duel—it contains now only the germs of double suicide.

Time was when victory in war represented a shortcut to power, a place in the sun, economic wealth and accelerated prosperity. It was the final weapon of statecraft; the apotheosis of political diplomacy. Its application, however, was regulated, controlled and limited by the basic principle that a great nation that entered upon war and did not see it through to victory would ultimately suffer all the consequences of defeat.

But the conditions that prevailed then exist no longer and will come no more. Once we were the sole possessors of nuclear power—we stood alone in military might. Now all this is changed. Others possess this weapon. Relative strengths from now on will probably change little with the years. Action by one will promptly be matched by reaction from the other.

The great question is, can global war now be outlawed from the world?

If so, it would mark the greatest advance in civilization since the Sermon on the Mount. It would lift at one stroke the darkest shadow which has engulfed mankind from the be-

ginning. It would not only remove fear and bring security—
it would not only create new moral and spiritual values—it
would produce an economic wave of prosperity that would
raise the world's standard of living beyond anything ever
dreamed of by man. The hundreds of billions of dollars
now spent in mutual preparedness could conceivably abolish
poverty from the face of the earth. It would accomplish
even more than this; it would at one stroke reduce the international tensions that seem to be insurmountable now to
matters of probable solution. This would not, of course,
mean the abandonment of all armed forces, but it would
reduce them to the simpler problems of internal order and
international police. It would not mean Utopia at one fell
stroke, but it would mean that the great roadblock now
existing to the development of the human race would have
been cleared.

You will say at once that although the abolition of war
has been the dream of man for centuries every proposition
to that end has been promptly discarded as impossible and
fantastic. But that was before the science of the past decade
made mass destruction a reality. The argument then was
along spiritual and moral lines, and lost. But now the tremendous evolution of nuclear and other potentials of destruction has suddenly taken the problem away from its
primary consideration as a moral and spiritual question and
brought it abreast of scientific realism. It is no longer an
ethical equation to be pondered solely by learned philosophers and ecclesiastics but a hard core one for the decision
of the masses whose survival is the issue. This is as true of
the Soviet side of the world as of the free side—as true
behind the Iron Curtain as in front of it. The ordinary
people of the world, such as you and I, whether free or slave,
are all in agreement on this solution; and this, perhaps, is

the only thing in the world they do agree upon, but it is the most vital and decisive of all. We are told that we must go on indefinitely as at present—with what at the end none say —there is no definite objective. The search for a final solution is but passed along to those who follow and, at the end, the problem will be exactly that which we face now.

It may take another cataclysm of destruction to prove the bald truth that the further evolution of civilization cannot take place until global war is abolished. This is the one issue upon which both sides can agree, for it is the one issue upon which both sides will profit equally. It is the one issue in which the interests of both are completely parallel. It is the one issue which, if settled, might settle all others.

The present tensions with their threat of national annihilation are fostered by two great illusions. The one a complete belief on the part of the Soviet world that the capitalistic countries are preparing to attack them eventually; that sooner or later we intend to strike. And the other, a complete belief on the part of the capitalistic countries that the Soviets are preparing to attack us; that sooner or later they intend to strike. Both are wrong. Each side, so far as the masses are concerned, is desirous of peace. Both dread war. But the constant acceleration of preparation may, without specific intent, ultimately precipitate a kind of spontaneous combustion.

Many will tell you, with mockery and ridicule, that the abolition of war can be only a dream—that it is but the vague imaginings of a visionary. But we must go on or we will go under. Their criticism is that the world has no plan which will enable us to go on. We have suffered the blood and the sweat and the tears. Now we seek the way and the truth and the light. We are in a new era. The old methods and solutions for this vital problem no longer suffice. We must have new thoughts, new ideas, new concepts. We must break out of the strait jacket of the past. We must have sufficient imagination and moral courage to translate this universal wish—which is rapidly becoming a universal necessity —into actuality. And until then we must be fully prepared, whatever the cost or sacrifice, lest we perish.

DOUGLAS MACARTHUR, General of the Army, has been Pro-Consul of the United States in postwar Japan, Marshal of the Philippines and Korean War commander. Since 1952, he has served as Chairman of the Board of Remington Rand, Inc. (to 1955) and of the Sperry Rand Corporation.

THE UNITED STATES
AND THE WORLD

Grayson Kirk

WE live in a time, not to try men's souls, but to try men's judgment. Confusion and uncertainty characterize our attitudes toward our national problems at home and abroad. We are warned that T. S. Eliot was wrong, and the world, our world, may soon end with an atomic bang almost equal to the galactic explosion in which it may have been born. We are told by others that our society is decaying at the core, and we are given as evidence such trends as the noxious growth of juvenile delinquency, apathy and corruption in public office, the callous disregard of public welfare by selfish special-interest groups, and the softness of our generation content to seek no more in life than what is euphemistically called leisure. As if this were not enough, we hear from others that our country has lost its safe mooring in economic and political policies and is drifting helplessly into socialism.

From our friends abroad we hear that this country is really not qualified by reasons of its tradition, temperament and the clumsiness of its central political structure to assume the exacting role of free-world leadership. And from unfriendly quarters abroad we hear the boast that, no matter what we do, our Ship of State is destined to break up on the rocks of historical inevitability.

With all these graduates of the Cassandra Institute lecturing us, it is little wonder that we are confused and apprehensive. Philosophically, we may find some comfort in the thought that, though our society is admittedly far from perfect, the same could be said in justice about every society of the past or present. And we may agree with Artsybashev that even if we were living in what comparatively might be called a Golden Age, we would not recognize it as such because we would have achieved it by such slow stages that we would have no perspective for judgment.

But no one is actually satisfied by such answers. And so we search desperately for a formula, a panacea, that will clear the atmosphere at home and abroad, and will relieve us of our fears. If you feel that I am overstating this sense of drift and confusion among our people, I would remind you that we have had but recently an official commission to tell us what our national goals should be. Is this not, in itself, a symptom of a deep-seated national malaise?

There was a time in the youth of our nation when we talked boldly about our Manifest Destiny. Today, in the midst of our worry, we still cling to the vestiges of that dream, but we are not really sure what our destiny is, or even what it ought to be. And it is not "manifest" to anyone.

Of all our concerns, the greatest is in the field of foreign affairs. The most casual cocktail-party remark of Chairman

Khrushchev will make the headlines from New York to San Francisco. We seem to have accepted the view that either the Soviet system or the one we represent must triumph everywhere in the world. We try to man the barriers of containment around the globe. We cheer every gain, however small, and we are in a frenzy of worry over every setback we experience. The familiar colloquial question, "How are we doing?" sums up what has become a national obsession in foreign affairs.

Such a question can only be answered in terms of the end sought. If our end is merely national survival, and future prospects therefor, we are doing very well indeed. Barring accidents or the successful provocation of a third power, the two greatest antagonists have of necessity such respect for each other's capabilities that they can no longer consider the use of major force as an available instrumentality of power with respect to each other. The rules, of course, will be changed when the atomic club has more members, but we have some years of respite before this becomes a current policy consideration.

But survival alone is not enough to satisfy us. We ask ourselves constantly where we stand with respect to the attitude of the remainder of the world. Should we try to buy more friendship with more aid? How do we make other peoples understand and share our ideals? Are our ideals merely those of democracy and freedom, or do they also include the concepts of limited government and free enterprise? The questions are confusing and the answers unclear.

This is not the time, and assuredly not the occasion, for an appraisal of our current posture in the world. But I will suggest three qualities we must have if we are to resolve our doubts, develop sound policies and gain greater confidence as we look to the future. Of themselves, they will not destroy our adversaries. In themselves they may hold a clue to the exit from our labyrinth.

The first quality we need is an increased objectivity in our judgments of other peoples. Different human societies do have different goals, and we must be wary of using ourselves as a measuring stick for others, and still more wary of imposing our own specific institutions upon them. What we tritely call "The American Way of Life" must not be a contemporary version of "The White Man's Burden" or of what the French once called "la mission civilisatrice." Montaigne made the point four centuries ago in his essay *Of Cannibals* when he remarked that ". . . each man calls barbarism whatever is not his own practice, for indeed it seems we have no other test of truth and reason than the example and pattern of the opinions and customs of the country we live in." And he added in his essay *Of Friendship* that "It is a dangerous and fateful presumption, besides the absurd temerity that it implies, to disdain what we do not comprehend." In a world rife with nationalism, we will succeed in our policies only if we replace all vestiges of condescension with sympathetic, though hardheaded, understanding.

The second quality is a greater awareness of the move and flow of history. Many a schoolboy who once recited in stumbling Latin the ancient aphorism that times change and we change with them grows up to be a confirmed, if unavowed, disciple of King Canute. Just as an individual of means and status is repelled by the prospect of drastic change in his life, so an opulent nation comes unconsciously to believe that the status quo, from which it has benefited, must be the best for everyone.

But this is not the way of history. At any given time many men and nations may demand change, even violent change, because they believe that their aspirations will not be satisfied by lesser measures. And at no time in history have so many peoples embraced a level of expectations beyond that which can be achieved by slow evolutionary processes.

The wise nation does attempt to influence these tides in the affairs of men in a fashion that will be favorable, or at least not unfavorable, to itself, but it recognizes clearly the folly of blind resistance to all change just because it is change. A wise people will judge movements and events, not as isolated or unique phenomena, but as external symptoms of deep-seated causes. Thus, as example, a wise people will not dismiss Castro's Cuba as a regrettable incident of comic-opera megalomania or even a painful case study in the technique of Communist infiltration. On the contrary, it examines the root-causes that suddenly grew such strange and bitter fruit; it estimates similar possibilities elsewhere; and it shapes judgments and policies accordingly. Neither history nor time is on the side of anyone, but wisdom based upon history is.

The third quality we need for more than bare survival, and quite possibly for survival itself, is an awareness of the inherent limitations of a free society. Being free, our weaknesses as well as our strengths are fully exposed to the world. Therefore, to an extent not shared by an authoritarian regime, the world has an opportunity to judge us by what we are and not by what we say we are. It behooves us, in consequence, to do everything in our power to set our own house in order, so that others may observe and approve. Justice and equality for all must be a working principle of our national life and not merely a motto carved over the door to a courtroom. Unless we practice what we preach, our preaching will win few converts. In the fiercely competitive world of today, an unfree nation may successfully conceal its imperfections; we have no choice but to make the most strenuous efforts to eliminate our own.

THE UNITED STATES AND THE WORLD

We must demonstrate to curious, skeptical, even unfriendly observers that our system can produce—and has produced—a society worthy of respect, friendship, and possibly emulation. If we permit ourselves to be regarded as soft, indolent, luxury-seeking and selfish, we will inspire no one to listen to us. If groups of our citizens openly ignore the general welfare in favor of selfish advantage, and manifest no overriding concern for the nation's economy or even its security, then all our fine words to the world will have a hollow ring. Self-discipline is hard for any people to learn, but without it no great nation can be free and no free nation can be great.

We must understand that the future of this country will be determined more by the wisdom and discipline of its citizens than by the vast physical power at their disposal.

GRAYSON KIRK is the fourteenth president of Columbia University. Dr. Kirk, internationally known educator and specialist in foreign affairs, is also a director of International Business Machines, Socony Vacuum, Inc., and other corporations, as well as author of *Philippine Independence, Contemporary International Politics* (with R. P. Stebbins) and many articles.